SEBA TWELL

32 G+ PROTEIN PER SERVING

HIGH PROTEIN COOKBOOK

120+ EASY LOW CARB RECIPES FOR WEIGHT LOSS, MUSCLE BUILDING, MEAL PREP & **GLP-1** DIET

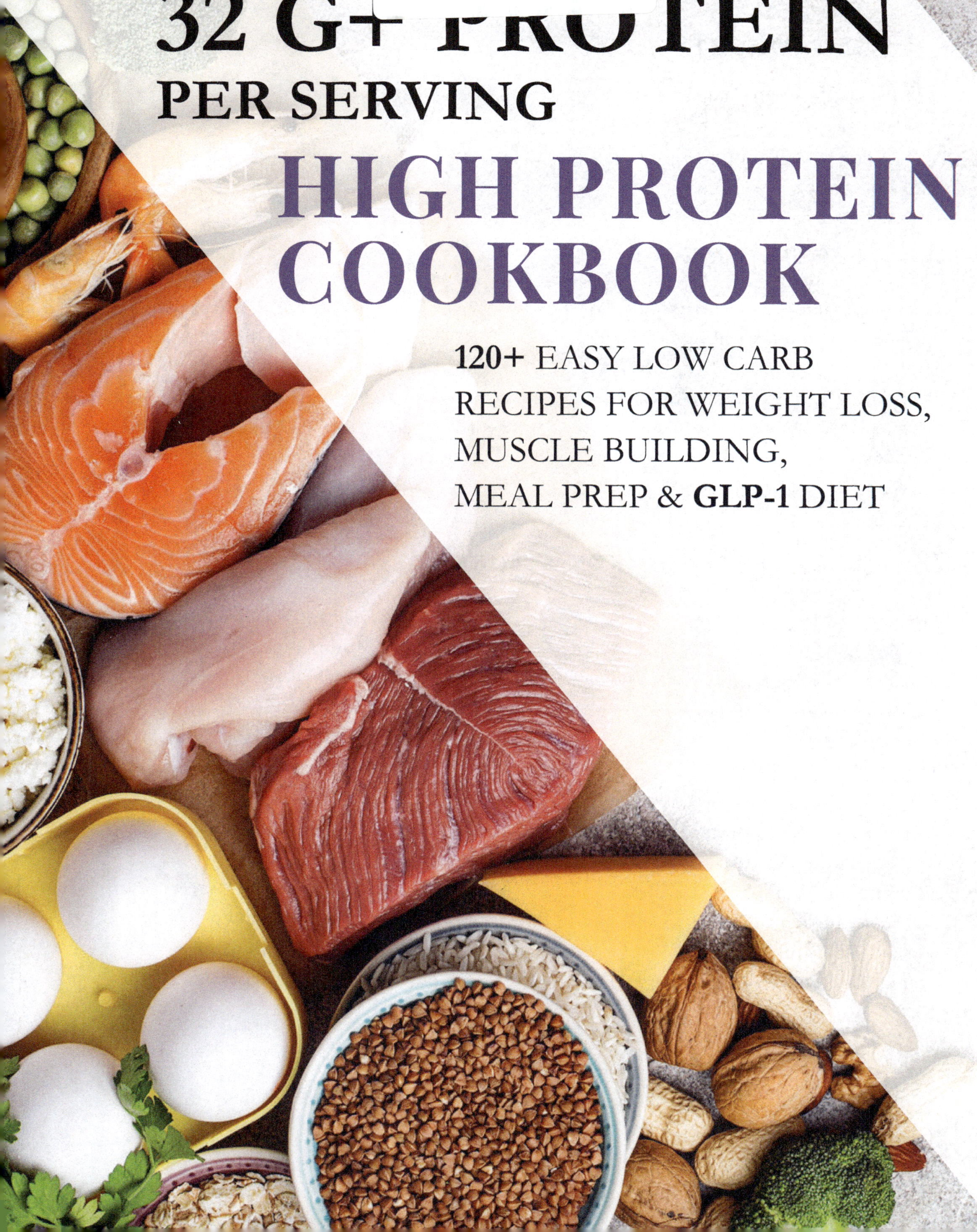

TABLE OF CONTENT

INTRODUCTION

WELCOME TO A REVOLUTION IN YOUR KITCHEN.

If you're holding this book, you are likely tired of the endless cycle of bland "health food," confusing diet plans, and meals that leave you hungry and unsatisfied. You're looking for a way to eat that is not only delicious and exciting but also delivers real, measurable results—whether your goal is to build lean muscle, shed body fat, or simply feel more energetic and powerful every single day.

You've come to the right place.

This Book is for You

This book is for the busy professional who needs energy to power through long days. It's for the athlete and the gym-goer who demand optimal fuel for performance and recovery. It's for the home cook who is passionate about flavor but serious about health. It's for anyone who has ever believed that healthy eating has to be a sacrifice. I'm here to tell you it doesn't.

THE HIGH-PROTEIN REVOLUTION

For decades, we were told to fear fat and count every calorie, while protein was often treated as an afterthought. The result? Meals that digest quickly, spike our blood sugar, and leave us craving more just an hour later.

The high-protein revolution is about flipping that script. It's a shift towards building every meal around a substantial, satisfying protein serving. This single change is the most powerful lever you can pull to transform your body composition, stabilize your energy levels, and take control of your hunger. It's not a diet; it's a sustainable lifestyle built on the principle of eating better, not less.

HOW TO USE THIS BOOK FOR MAXIMUM RESULTS

This isn't just a collection of recipes; it's a complete system for success. Here's how to get the most out of it:

1. **Trust the Numbers:** Every recipe in this book has been meticulously designed to deliver at least 32 grams of protein per serving. We've done the hard work for you. Simply pick a recipe, and you can be confident it's hitting your protein target.
2. **Embrace the Philosophy:** We've organized this book by protein source (Chicken, Beef, Fish, etc.), not by cuisine. Read "The Protein Source Philosophy" on page 10 to understand how this will revolutionize your shopping and meal prep.
3. **Customize Your Carbs:** Your goals are unique, and your meals should be too. On page 13, you'll find our "Carb Substitution System." This powerful tool lets you tailor any recipe to your specific carbohydrate needs, from ultra-low-carb to performance-focused.
4. **One Recipe, One Serving:** Remember, every recipe is designed to be one generous, single serving. This makes tracking your intake effortless. If you're cooking for two, just double the ingredients.

Prepare to feel stronger, leaner, and more satisfied than ever before. Let's start cooking.

Quick Reference: All recipes in this book are designed for single servings. Multiply ingredients by the number of people you're feeding.

THE SCIENCE OF PROTEIN

Why the obsession with protein? And why the specific number—32 grams? The answers lie in science. Understanding the "why" will empower you to stick with this way of eating for the long term.

Why Exactly 32+ Grams of Protein?

Modern research has revealed a "protein threshold" for muscle protein synthesis (MPS)—the process by which the body repairs and builds muscle tissue. Studies show that a meal containing approximately 30-40 grams of high-quality protein is optimal to maximize this response. Consuming less may not provide a strong enough signal to trigger significant muscle repair, while consuming much more in a single sitting doesn't seem to offer additional muscle-building benefits.

Our target of 32 grams or more per serving places every meal squarely in this optimal zone. It ensures that, whether you're coming from a workout or just living your life, you are giving your body the powerful signal it needs to maintain and build lean tissue —the metabolic engine of your body.

Protein and Your Metabolism

Protein has the highest Thermic Effect of Food (TEF) of all macronutrients. This means your body burns more calories digesting protein than it does digesting fats or carbohydrates. Up to 30% of the calories from protein are used just for its digestion and processing! This gives your metabolism a natural boost with every meal. Furthermore, by preserving and building muscle mass, you increase your resting metabolic rate—the number of calories you burn just by being alive.

Protein for Different Goals

- **For Weight Loss:** Protein is your greatest ally. It is incredibly satiating, meaning it keeps you feeling full and satisfied for longer, dramatically reducing cravings and overall calorie intake. Preserving muscle mass during a calorie deficit ensures you are losing fat, not valuable muscle.
- **For Muscle Gain:** To build muscle, you need a positive protein balance—meaning you must synthesize more muscle protein than you break down. Hitting the 30-40g protein target at each meal provides the essential building blocks (amino acids) and the signal (leucine) needed for growth and development.
- **For Maintenance & Healthy Aging:** As we age, we naturally lose muscle mass (a condition called sarcopenia). Consistently eating adequate protein is the single most effective nutritional strategy to combat this, preserving strength, mobility, and metabolic health for years to come.

Complete vs. Incomplete Proteins

A "complete" protein contains all nine essential amino acids that your body cannot produce on its own. Animal sources, such as meat, fish, eggs, and dairy, are all complete proteins. Most plant proteins are "incomplete," but this is easily solved by combining different sources (like beans and rice). In this book, we focus on high-quality, complete protein sources to ensure every meal is as effective as possible.

THE PROTEIN SOURCE PHILOSOPHY

This cookbook is organized differently. Instead of chapters like "Italian Food" or "Asian Food," you'll see sections like "Chicken," "Beef," "Fish & Seafood," and "Plant-Based." This is a deliberate choice designed for one purpose: to make your life easier.

Why Not Organize by World Cuisines?

A traditional cookbook structure forces you into a scattered shopping experience. On Monday, you need chicken for an Italian dish, on Tuesday, you need lamb for an Indian dish, and on Wednesday, you need fish for a Mexican dish. This is inefficient, expensive, and leads to food waste.

Practicality for Shopping and Planning

Our system is built around the way you actually shop and plan. You can buy a value pack of chicken breasts or ground beef for the week, then flip to the corresponding chapter and find a world of variety. You'll have five different, exciting ways to cook that one core ingredient, from an Asian-inspired stir-fry to a Mediterranean-style grill.

International Variety Within Each Section

This structure doesn't sacrifice flavor or variety—it enhances it. The "Chicken" chapter isn't just five ways to grill a chicken breast. It's a culinary journey. You'll find a recipe for Indian Chicken Tikka Masala right next to a Greek Lemon-Herb Chicken and a Spicy Thai Basil Chicken. You get global flavors with a streamlined, practical approach.

How This Simplifies Meal Prep

This philosophy is a game-changer for meal prep. You can cook a large batch of your core protein (e.g., shredded chicken, ground turkey) on Sunday. Then, throughout the week, you can quickly assemble different meals using that pre-cooked protein.

- Monday: Use the shredded chicken in a high-protein "Greek Island" Salad.
- Tuesday: Reheat the chicken with the sauce for our Low-Carb Tikka Masala.
- Wednesday: Mix it with black beans and spices for a quick Chicken Chili.

This "cook once, eat three ways" method saves you hours in the kitchen and ensures you never get bored. It's the ultimate fusion of efficiency and flavor.

THE FIBER & CARB SYSTEM

Protein is our hero, but fiber is its essential partner. A high-protein diet is only truly effective and healthy when paired with adequate fiber. At the same time, carbohydrate needs vary widely. This chapter presents a straightforward yet effective system for managing both.

Why Fiber is Critically Important

Fiber is the unsung hero of digestive health, blood sugar stability, and satiety. It feeds your gut microbiome, slows down digestion (keeping you fuller for longer), and prevents the blood sugar spikes that can lead to energy crashes and fat storage. A diet rich in protein and fiber is the ideal combination for regulating appetite and promoting metabolic health.

Our Fiber-First Approach & The 8-Gram Rule

While our main dishes are optimized for protein, fiber primarily comes from the side dishes you pair them with. We've designed our system around a simple but powerful guideline:

The 8-Gram Rule: We strongly recommend pairing every main dish with sides that ensure your total meal contains at least 8 grams of fiber.

Our "Carb Substitution System" below is built on this principle. By choosing a side from Level 1 (like a large portion of leafy greens) or Level 2 (like roasted broccoli), you will easily meet and often exceed this fiber target. This approach transforms a great high-protein dish into a perfectly balanced, satisfying meal.

The Carb Substitution System (4 Levels)

Your daily carb needs depend on your activity level and goals. This flexible system allows you to tailor any recipe by choosing the right side dish.

- **Level 1:** Ultra Low-Carb (<15g Carbs per Meal) | Fiber-Rich Foundation
  - How: Serve the main dish with a generous portion of: cauliflower rice, zucchini noodles, steamed spinach, or a large mixed green salad.
  - Best for: Keto diets and initial fat-loss phases.
- **Level 2:** Low-Carb (<30g Carbs per Meal) | Vegetable Power
  - Serve with a hearty portion of roasted low-carb vegetables, such as broccoli, bell peppers, asparagus, or Brussels sprouts.
  - Best for: General fat loss, moderate activity levels.
- **Level 3:** Moderate-Carb (<50g Carbs per Meal) | Complex Carbs
  - How: Add a small portion (1/2 cup cooked) of a high-fiber carbohydrate like quinoa, chickpeas, lentils, or black beans.
  - Best for: Muscle gain phases, pre-workout meals.
- **Level 4:** High-Carb (50g+ Carbs per Meal) | Performance Fuel
  - How: Add a full portion (1 cup cooked) of complex carbs like sweet potato, brown rice, or oats.
  - Best for: Post-workout recovery for intense athletes, endurance training.

How to Adapt Recipes to Your Goals

It's simple. Prepare the main protein dish exactly as described. Then, look at your goal for the day and choose your carb level, knowing it will also help you meet your fiber target. This system puts you in the driver's seat, making this book a lifelong tool for your health and fitness journey.

EGGS

Welcome to the most versatile protein source in the world. Eggs are the ultimate nutritional powerhouse: affordable, quick to cook, and packed with high-quality amino acids. In this chapter, we elevate the humble egg from a simple breakfast food to a high-protein star suitable for any meal of the day. Each recipe is engineered to be a complete, satisfying dish that meets our 32-gram protein promise.

GREEK SPINACH & FETA FRITTATA

Method

1. Preheat oven to 400°F (200°C).
2. In an oven-safe skillet, sauté the onion in oil. Add spinach and cook until wilted.
3. In a bowl, whisk eggs, yogurt, dill, salt, and pepper.
4. Pour the egg mixture over the spinach. Sprinkle feta on top.
5. Cook on the stovetop for 2-3 minutes, until the edges are set. Then,. Then, transfer the dish to the oven and bake for 10-12 minutes or until fully set.

Ingredients

- Eggs: 5 large
- Feta Cheese, crumbled: 60g / 2 oz
- Spinach, chopped: 100g / 3.5 oz
- Onion, finely chopped: 1/4
- Full-Fat Greek Yogurt: 2 tbsp
- Dill, chopped; salt, pepper.
- Olive Oil: 1 tsp

Macros

~ 450 kcal | P: 38g | F: 30g | C: 8g

TURKISH MENEMEN WITH SUJUK

Method

1. In a skillet, sauté the onion and pepper in oil. Add sujuk/chorizo and cook until it releases its oils.
2. Add tomato and spices. Simmer for 5-7 mins until a thick sauce forms.
3. Make wells in the sauce and crack the eggs directly into them.
4. Cover and cook on low heat for 5-7 minutes, until the egg whites are set but the yolks are still runny.
5. Garnish with fresh parsley.

Ingredients

- Eggs: 4 large
- Sujuk (spicy Turkish sausage) or Chorizo, sliced: 60g / 2 oz
- Tomato, chopped: 1 large
- Green Bell Pepper, chopped: 1/2
- Onion, chopped: 1/4
- Spices: Paprika, red pepper flakes.
- Olive Oil: 1 tbsp

Macros

~ 450 kcal | P: 38g | F: 30g | C: 8g

HIGH-PROTEIN AMERICAN EGG MUFFINS

Method

1. Preheat oven to 375°F (190°C). Grease a 4-cup muffin tin.
2. In a bowl, whisk eggs and cottage cheese until smooth.
3. Stir in the chopped bacon/ham, cheddar, bell pepper, and green onion.
4. Divide the mixture evenly among the four muffin cups.
5. Bake for 20-25 mins until puffed, golden, and set in the center.

Ingredients

- Eggs: 6 large
- Cottage Cheese (full-fat): 100g / 3.5 oz
- Cooked Bacon or Ham, chopped: 60g / 2 oz
- Cheddar Cheese, shredded: 40g / 1.5 oz
- Bell Pepper, finely diced: 1/4
- Green Onion, sliced.

Macros

~480 kcal | P: 40g | F: 32g | C: 8g

INDIAN EGG CURRY (ANDHRA-STYLE)

Method

1. Peel the hard-boiled eggs and make small slits in the whites.
2. In a pan, sauté the onion in ghee until golden. Add ginger-garlic paste and spices, cook for 1 min.
3. Add tomato and cook until it breaks down into a sauce.
4. Reduce the heat to low. Slowly stir in the whisked yogurt. Do not boil.
5. Gently add the eggs to the sauce and simmer for 5 mins. Garnish with cilantro.

Ingredients

- Hard-Boiled Eggs: 4
- Full-Fat Greek Yogurt: 100g / 3.5 oz
- Onion, finely chopped: 1/2
- Tomato, chopped: 1
- Ginger-Garlic Paste: 1 tsp
- Spices: Turmeric, chili powder, coriander, cumin.
- Ghee or Coconut Oil: 1 tbsp

Macros

~500 kcal | P: 32g | F: 38g | C: 12g

FRENCH HERB OMELET WITH GRUYÈRE

Method

1. In a bowl, whisk eggs, cream, salt, and pepper until just combined (do not over-beat). Stir in the fresh herbs.
2. Heat butter in a non-stick skillet over medium heat.
3. Pour in the egg mixture. As the edges set, gently push them toward the center, tilting the pan to let the uncooked egg flow underneath.
4. When the omelet is nearly set, sprinkle the cheese over one half.
5. Fold the other half over the cheese and slide it onto a plate.

Ingredients

- Eggs: 5 large
- Gruyère or Swiss Cheese, shredded: 60g / 2 oz
- Heavy Cream: 1 tbsp
- Fresh Herbs, finely chopped (chives, parsley, tarragon): 2 tbsp
- Butter: 1 tbsp
- Salt and white pepper.

Macros

~490 kcal | P: 38g | F: 36g | C: 5g

MEXICAN HUEVOS RANCHEROS BOWL

Method

1. In a skillet, cook the chorizo/beef. Add the black soybeans and salsa, and heat through to a simmer.
2. In a separate pan, fry the eggs in oil to your liking (sunny-side up is traditional).
3. Place the chorizo-bean mixture in a bowl. Top with the fried eggs.
4. Garnish with sliced avocado and crumbled cheese.

Ingredients

- Eggs: 4 large
- Chorizo or Ground Beef: 60g / 2 oz
- Black Soybeans, rinsed: 80g / 2.8 oz
- Salsa (low-sugar): 3 tbsp
- Avocado, sliced: 1/2
- Cotija or Feta Cheese, crumbled: 30g / 1 oz
- Oil: 1 tsp

Macros

~540 kcal | P: 34g | F: 38g | C: 15g

ITALIAN ZUCCHINI & PARMESAN FRITTATA

Method

1. Preheat oven to 400°F (200°C).
2. In an oven-safe skillet, sauté onion and garlic in oil. Add zucchini and cook until tender and lightly browned.
3. In a bowl, whisk together the eggs, ricotta, half of the Parmesan, salt, and pepper.
4. Pour the egg mixture over the zucchini. Sprinkle the remaining Parmesan on top.
5. Cook on the stovetop for 2-3 minutes, then bake for 10-12 minutes, until set.

Ingredients

- Eggs: 5 large
- Zucchini, thinly sliced: 1 small
- Parmesan Cheese, grated: 40g / 1.5 oz
- Ricotta Cheese: 2 tbsp
- Garlic, minced: 1 clove
- Onion, chopped: 1/4
- Olive Oil: 1 tbsp

Macros

~460 kcal | P: 36g | F: 32g | C: 9g

THAI-STYLE PORK & HERB OMELET (KAI JEOW MOO SAB)

Method

1. In a bowl, whisk eggs with fish sauce until frothy. Add the ground pork, green onion, and cilantro, and mix until well combined.
2. Heat oil in a wok or small skillet over medium-high heat until very hot.
3. Pour the egg mixture into the hot oil. It should puff up dramatically.
4. Cook for 2-3 mins per side, until golden brown and crispy on the outside and the pork is cooked through.
5. Serve immediately, typically accompanied by a side of cucumber.

Ingredients

- Eggs: 4 large
- Ground Pork: 80g / 2.8 oz
- Fish Sauce: 2 tsp
- Green Onion, sliced: 1
- Cilantro, chopped.
- Avocado Oil or other high-heat oil: 2 tbsp

Macros

~510 kcal | P: 35g | F: 40g | C: 4g

MOROCCAN SHAKSHUKA WITH MERGUEZ SAUSAGE

Method

1. In a skillet, brown the sausage, breaking it into small pieces. Add the onion and pepper, and cook until they are soft.
2. Add spices and cook for 1 min. Pour in the crushed tomatoes.
3. Simmer for 10 mins until the sauce thickens.
4. Make wells in the sauce and crack the eggs in. Sprinkle feta around the eggs.
5. Cover and cook on low for 5-8 mins until egg whites are set.

Ingredients

- Eggs: 4 large
- Merguez (lamb sausage) or Chorizo, casing removed: 80g / 2.8 oz
- Crushed Tomatoes: 250g / 8.8 oz
- Bell Pepper, chopped: 1/2
- Onion, chopped: 1/4
- Spices: Cumin, smoked paprika, coriander, and a pinch of cayenne.
- Feta Cheese, crumbled: 30g / 1 oz

Macros

~530 kcal | P: 36g | F: 38g | C: 14g

JAPANESE ROLLED OMELET WITH CHEESE (TAMAGOYAKI)

Method

1. In a bowl, whisk eggs, blended cottage cheese, and soy sauce.
2. Heat a rectangular tamagoyaki pan (or a small non-stick skillet) over medium heat and lightly oil it.
3. Pour in a thin layer of the egg mixture. When it's nearly set, sprinkle with some cheese and green onion.
4. From the far end, gently roll the omelet toward you.
5. Push the rolled omelet back to the far end. Oil the empty part of the pan and pour in another thin layer of egg, letting it flow under the roll.
6. Repeat the rolling and layering process until all the egg mixture is used. Slide onto a cutting board and slice.

Ingredients

- Eggs: 5 large
- Cottage Cheese, blended smooth: 3 tbsp
- Shredded Mozzarella or Provolone: 40g / 1.5 oz
- Soy Sauce (or tamari): 1 tsp
- Green Onion, finely chopped.
- Oil for cooking.

Macros

~440 kcal | P: 34g | F: 32g | C: 6g

CHICKEN & TURKEY

Chicken and turkey are the cornerstones of any high-protein diet. They are lean, versatile, and incredibly efficient at delivering the amino acids your body needs. This chapter is a global tour designed to prove that you never have to eat a boring "grilled chicken breast" again. From spicy Asian stir-fries to rich European classics, every recipe transforms this everyday protein into an extraordinary meal.

JAPANESE TERIYAKI CHICKEN

Method

1. In a bowl, mix all sauce ingredients.
2. Pan-sear chicken thighs in hot oil for 4-5 mins per side until cooked through and crispy.
3. Lower the heat, pour the sauce over the chicken. Simmer for 2-3 mins until the sauce thickens and glazes the chicken.
4. Garnish with sesame seeds and green onions. Serve with steamed broccoli.

Ingredients

- Chicken Thighs, boneless, skinless: 220g / 8 oz
- Sauce: Soy Sauce (or Tamari): 3 tbsp; Swerve/Erythritol: 1 tbsp; Sake/Mirin: 1 tbsp; Grated Ginger & Garlic.
- Avocado Oil: 1 tsp

Macros

~480 kcal | P: 45g | F: 28g | C: 10g

GREEK CHICKEN GYROS

Method

1. Marinate chicken for at least 20 mins.
2. In a hot skillet, cook chicken until golden and cooked through.
3. Mix all tzatziki ingredients. Chop the salad vegetables.
4. Serve the hot chicken in a bowl topped with fresh salad and a large dollop of tzatziki.

Ingredients

- Chicken Breast, thinly sliced: 200g / 7 oz
- Marinade: Olive oil, lemon juice, oregano, and garlic powder.
- Tzatziki Sauce: Greek Yogurt (100g); grated cucumber, dill, garlic.
- Salad: Cucumber, tomato, red onion.

Macros

~520 kcal | P: 48g | F: 32g | C: 12g

MEXICAN CHICKEN FAJITAS

Method

1. Toss chicken with half the spice mix.
2. In a hot skillet, heat oil and cook chicken until browned. Remove from the pan.
3. Add peppers and onion to the same pan, sauté until tender-crisp.
4. Return chicken to the pan, add remaining spices, and toss to combine.
5. Serve hot with low-carb tortillas or on a bed of lettuce with salsa and Greek yogurt.

Ingredients

- Chicken Breast, sliced: 200g / 7 oz
- Bell Peppers (mixed colors), sliced: 1 cup
- Onion, sliced: 1/2
- Spice Mix: Chili powder, cumin, paprika, and garlic powder.
- Avocado Oil: 1 tbsp

Macros

~490 kcal | P: 45g | F: 28g | C: 14g

ITALIAN CHICKEN PARMESAN (LOW-CARB)

Method

1. Preheat oven to 425°F (220°C).
2. Dip chicken in beaten egg, then press into the almond flour/Parmesan mixture to coat.
3. Pan-sear the chicken in oil for 2-3 mins per side until golden.
4. Place on a baking sheet, top with marinara and mozzarella.
5. Bake for 10-12 minutes, or until the cheese is bubbly and the chicken is cooked through. Serve with zucchini noodles.

Ingredients

- Chicken Breast, pounded thin: 200g / 7 oz
- Breading: Almond Flour (3 tbsp); grated Parmesan (2 tbsp).
- Egg, beaten: 1
- Marinara Sauce (low-sugar): 3 tbsp
- Mozzarella Cheese, sliced: 40g / 1.5 oz

Macros

~550 kcal | P: 50g | F: 35g | C: 12g

INDIAN TANDOORI CHICKEN

Method

1. Make deep cuts in the chicken meat.
2. In a bowl, combine all marinade ingredients. Thoroughly coat the chicken, pushing the marinade into the cuts. Marinate for at least 2 hours (or overnight).
3. Preheat oven/air fryer to 400°F (200°C).
4. Bake for 25-30 mins, turning halfway, until cooked through and charred in spots.
5. Serve with a mint-yogurt sauce and cucumber salad.

Ingredients

- Chicken Leg & Thigh, skinless: 250g / 8.8 oz
- Marinade: Greek Yogurt (100g); Tandoori Masala paste (2 tbsp); ginger-garlic paste; lemon juice.

Macros

~480 kcal | P: 48g | F: 28g | C: 9g

THAI LARB GAI
(CHICKEN SALAD)

Method

1. In a dry, non-stick pan, cook the ground chicken over medium heat, breaking it up, until it is cooked through. Drain any excess liquid.
2. In a bowl, combine the hot chicken with all dressing ingredients and the shallot.
3. Let it sit for 5 minutes to allow the flavors to absorb.
4. Stir in the fresh herbs and red pepper flakes. Serve warm in lettuce cups.

Ingredients

- Ground Chicken or Turkey: 200g / 7 oz
- Dressing: Lime Juice (3 tbsp); Fish Sauce (2 tbsp); Swerve/Erythritol (1 tsp).
- Shallot, thinly sliced: 1
- Fresh Mint & Cilantro, chopped: 1/2 cup
- Red Pepper Flakes, to taste.

Macros

~450 kcal | P: 42g | F: 28g | C: 8g

AMERICAN BBQ CHICKEN
(LOW-SUGAR)

Method

1. Preheat grill or oven to 400°F (200°C). Season chicken with salt and pepper.
2. In a small bowl, whisk all BBQ sauce ingredients.
3. Grill or bake chicken for 15 mins.
4. Brush a generous layer of BBQ sauce over the chicken. Cook for an additional 5-10 minutes, turning and basting as needed, until the meat is caramelized and cooked through.
5. Serve with a side of coleslaw dressed with yogurt.

Ingredients

- Chicken Breast or Thighs: 220g / 8 oz
- BBQ Sauce: Tomato Paste (2 tbsp); Apple Cider Vinegar (2 tbsp); Smoked Paprika (1 tsp); Garlic Powder; Swerve/Erythritol to taste.

Macros

~490 kcal | P: 46g | F: 30g | C: 10g

LEBANESE CHICKEN SHAWARMA BOWL

Method

1. Marinate chicken for at least 30 mins.
2. Cook the chicken in a hot skillet until it is browned and cooked through.
3. Mix the garlic sauce ingredients.
4. Serve the chicken in a bowl over shredded lettuce. Top with pickled turnips (low-carb) and a generous amount of garlic sauce.

Ingredients

- Chicken Thighs, sliced: 220g / 8 oz
- Marinade: Olive oil, lemon juice, cumin, coriander, paprika, turmeric, and garlic.
- Garlic Sauce (Toum): Greek Yogurt (100g); 2-3 cloves minced garlic; lemon juice.

Macros

~530 kcal | P: 48g | F: 34g | C: 11g

RUSSIAN TURKEY CUTLETS (KOTLETI)

Method

1. In a bowl, mix ground turkey, grated onion, egg, dill, salt, and pepper until just combined. Do not overmix.
2. Form the mixture into 2-3 oval patties.
3. Lightly coat each patty in the crushed pork rinds.
4. Pan-fry in ghee over medium heat for 5-7 mins per side, until golden brown and cooked through.
5. Serve with sautéed mushrooms or a simple salad.

Ingredients

- Ground Turkey: 220g / 8 oz
- Onion, grated: 1/4
- Egg: 1
- Pork Rinds, crushed (for breading): 1/4 cup
- Dill, chopped; salt, pepper.
- Ghee or Avocado Oil for frying.

Macros

~470 kcal | P: 45g | F: 30g | C: 5g

ARGENTINIAN CHIMICHURRI CHICKEN

Method

1. Grill or pan-sear the chicken breast until cooked through. Let it rest.
2. To make the sauce, finely chop the parsley and garlic (or use a food processor, but don't purée it).
3. In a bowl, combine the parsley-garlic mix with olive oil, vinegar, oregano, and red pepper flakes.
4. Slice the rested chicken breast. Serve topped with a generous amount of fresh chimichurri sauce.

Ingredients

- Chicken Breast: 200g / 7 oz
- Chimichurri Sauce: Fresh Parsley (1 cup); 3-4 cloves garlic; Olive Oil (3 tbsp); Red Wine Vinegar (2 tbsp); Dried Oregano; Red Pepper Flakes.

Macros

~510 kcal | P: 46g | F: 35g | C: 5g

GERMAN CHICKEN SCHNITZEL

Method

1. Season chicken with salt and pepper.
2. Dip chicken in egg, then press firmly into the almond flour/pork rind mixture.
3. Shallow-fry in hot ghee for 3-4 minutes per side, until deep golden brown and crispy.
4. Serve immediately with a lemon wedge and a simple green salad.

Ingredients

- Chicken Breast, pounded very thin: 200g / 7 oz
- Breading: Almond Flour (3 tbsp); crushed Pork Rinds (2 tbsp).
- Egg, beaten: 1
- Ghee or Avocado Oil for frying.

Macros

~510 kcal | P: 48g | F: 33g | C: 8g

KOREAN DAKGALBI (SPICY STIR-FRIED CHICKEN)

Method

1. Marinate chicken in the sauce for at least 15 mins.
2. In a large hot skillet, stir-fry the chicken for 5-7 minutes.
3. Add the cabbage and continue to stir-fry until the chicken is cooked and the cabbage is tender.
4. (Optional) Top with mozzarella, cover the pan, and let it melt for 1-2 mins.

Ingredients

- Chicken Thighs, cubed: 220g / 8 oz
- Cabbage, roughly chopped: 1 cup
- Sauce: Gochujang (Korean chili paste, 2 tbsp); Soy Sauce (1 tbsp); minced Garlic & Ginger.
- Mozzarella Cheese, shredded (optional): 30g / 1 oz

Macros

~500 kcal | P: 45g | F: 30g | C: 14g

FRENCH COQ AU VIN
(QUICK VERSION)

Method

1. In a pot, cook bacon until crisp. Remove bacon, leave fat.
2. Brown chicken thighs in the bacon fat. Add onion, garlic, and mushrooms; cook for 5 mins.
3. Pour in red wine to deglaze the pan. Add broth and return bacon to the pot.
4. Simmer for 25-30 mins until the chicken is tender and the sauce has reduced. Serve over cauliflower mash.

Ingredients

- Chicken Thighs: 250g / 8.8 oz
- Bacon or Pancetta, diced: 30g / 1 oz
- Mushrooms, sliced: 1/2 cup
- Dry Red Wine (like Burgundy): 1/2 cup
- Chicken Broth: 1/2 cup
- Onion & Garlic, chopped.

Macros

~540 kcal | P: 48g | F: 32g | C: 12g

CHINESE KUNG PAO CHICKEN
(LOW-CARB)

Method

1. In a hot wok or skillet, stir-fry the chicken in oil until it is browned.
2. Add garlic, ginger, and dried chilies; stir-fry for 30 seconds until fragrant.
3. Pour in the soy sauce and vinegar. Continue cooking until the sauce has glazed the chicken.
4. Stir in the roasted peanuts. Serve immediately with stir-fried bell peppers.

Ingredients

- Chicken Breast, cubed: 200g / 7 oz
- Dry-Roasted Peanuts: 30g / 1 oz
- Sauce: Soy Sauce (2 tbsp); Rice Vinegar (1 tbsp); minced Garlic & Ginger; a few dried red chilies.
- Avocado Oil: 1 tbsp

Macros

~520 kcal | P: 45g | F: 34g | C: 11g

CUBAN MOJO CHICKEN

Method

1. Combine all marinade ingredients. Marinate chicken for at least 1 hour.
2. Heat oil in a skillet. Sear the chicken for 5-6 minutes per side, until golden and cooked through.
3. Pour the remaining marinade into the pan and let it bubble and reduce to a glaze.
4. Serve the chicken topped with sautéed onions.

Ingredients

- Chicken Thighs: 250g / 8.8 oz
- Mojo Marinade: Orange Juice (1/4 cup, fresh squeezed); Lime Juice (1/4 cup); 4-5 cloves minced Garlic; dried Oregano; Cumin.
- Olive Oil: 1 tbsp

Macros

~500 kcal | P: 46g | F: 33g | C: 7g

MOROCCAN CHICKEN TAGINE (QUICK SKILLET VERSION)

Method

1. In a skillet, brown the chicken. Add onion and cook until soft.
2. Add garlic and all the spices, and cook for 1 minute.
3. Pour in the broth and bring to a simmer. Cover and cook for 20 mins.
4. Stir in the olives and preserved lemon. Cook for a final 5 mins. Garnish with fresh cilantro.

Ingredients

- Chicken Thighs, cubed: 220g / 8 oz
- Onion, chopped; Garlic, minced.
- Spices: Turmeric, cumin, ginger, cinnamon.
- Chicken Broth: 1/2 cup
- Green Olives, pitted: 1/4 cup
- Preserved Lemon, rind only, finely chopped: 1 tsp (optional)

Macros

~530 kcal | P: 48g | F: 30g | C: 15g

VIETNAMESE PHO GA
(BROTH BOWL)

Method

1. In a pot, simmer the broth with all aromatics for at least 15 minutes to infuse the broth with flavor.
2. Remove the solid aromatics from the broth.
3. Place zucchini noodles and bean sprouts in a large bowl. Top with the shredded chicken.
4. Pour the piping hot broth over everything. Serve immediately with a plate of fresh garnishes.

Ingredients

- Chicken Breast, cooked and shredded: 180g / 6.5 oz
- Chicken Broth (high quality): 2 cups
- Aromatics: Star Anise (1); Cinnamon Stick (1/2); Ginger slices.
- Garnish: Zucchini Noodles; Bean Sprouts; Fresh Basil, Cilantro, Lime, Jalapeño.

Macros

~450 kcal | P: 40g | F: 25g | C: 10g

ETHIOPIAN DORO WAT
(SPICY CHICKEN STEW)

Method

1. In a dry pot, cook the onion over low heat for 10-15 mins until soft and sweet.
2. Add ghee and Berbere spice, cook for 2 mins. Add garlic and ginger.
3. Add the chicken and a splash of water. Cover and simmer for 30-40 mins until chicken is very tender.
4. Add the hard-boiled egg to the stew for the last 5 mins to warm through.

Ingredients

- Chicken Thighs: 250g / 8.8 oz
- Hard-Boiled Egg, peeled: 1
- Onion, finely chopped: 1 large
- Berbere Spice Blend: 2 tbsp
- Ghee or Niter Kibbeh (spiced butter): 1 tbsp
- Garlic & Ginger, minced.

Macros

~520 kcal | P: 48g | F: 30g | C: 13g

AMERICAN BUFFALO WINGS
(BAKED)

Method

1. Preheat oven to 425°F (220°C).
2. Thoroughly pat wings dry with paper towels. Toss with baking powder, salt, and pepper.
3. Place on a wire rack over a baking sheet. Bake for 40-50 mins, flipping halfway, until deep golden and crispy.
4. Whisk hot sauce and melted butter. Toss the hot wings in the sauce to evenly coat them.

Ingredients

- Chicken Wings: 300g / 10.5 oz
- Baking Powder: 1 tsp (for crispiness)
- Buffalo Sauce: Frank's RedHot sauce (1/4 cup); Melted Butter (2 tbsp).
- Serve with: Celery sticks and blue cheese or ranch dressing.

Macros

~550 kcal | P: 45g | F: 40g | C: 5g

UKRAINIAN CHICKEN KIEV
(BAKED)

Method

1. Mix the filling ingredients, then form into a small log. Freeze for 15 mins.
2. Place the cold butter log in the center of the chicken breast, then wrap it tightly, sealing all edges.
3. Dip the chicken parcel in egg, then coat thoroughly in the almond/Parmesan breading.
4. Bake at 400°F (200°C) for 25-30 mins until golden and cooked through. Let rest for 5 mins before cutting.

Ingredients

- Chicken Breast, pounded very thin: 200g / 7 oz
- Filling: Cold Butter (2 tbsp), minced garlic, chopped dill, and parsley.
- Breading: Almond Flour (3 tbsp); grated Parmesan (2 tbsp).
- Egg, beaten: 1

Macros

~560 kcal | P: 50g | F: 38g | C: 8g

PERUVIAN POLLO A LA BRASA
(ROASTED CHICKEN)

Method

1. Combine all marinade ingredients. Marinate chicken for at least 2 hours.
2. Preheat oven or air fryer to 400°F (200°C).
3. Roast the chicken for 30-35 mins, skin-side up, until the skin is dark and crispy and the meat is cooked through.
4. Serve with a spicy green sauce (Aji Verde) made from cilantro, jalapeño, and Greek yogurt.

Ingredients

- Chicken Leg & Thigh, skin-on: 250g / 8.8 oz
- Marinade: Soy Sauce (2 tbsp); minced Garlic; Cumin; Paprika; Lime Juice; 1 tbsp oil.

Macros

~500 kcal | P: 48g | F: 32g | C: 6g

SPANISH "PAELLA" WITH CHICKEN & CHORIZO

Method

1. In a large skillet, brown the chicken and chorizo. Add the onion and pepper, and cook until they are soft.
2. Add paprika and saffron, stir for 30 seconds.
3. Stir in the cauliflower rice, coating it in the oils and spices.
4. Pour in the broth, bring to a simmer, then reduce the heat, cover, and cook for 10-12 mins until the cauliflower is tender.

Ingredients

- Chicken Thigh, cubed: 180g / 6.5 oz
- Spanish Chorizo, sliced: 40g / 1.5 oz
- Cauliflower Rice: 1.5 cups
- Bell Pepper & Onion, chopped.
- Spices: Smoked paprika, saffron threads.
- Chicken Broth: 1/2 cup

Macros

~540 kcal | P: 45g | F: 35g | C: 14g

BRAZILIAN CHICKEN FRICASSEE

Method

1. Preheat oven to 375°F (190°C).
2. In a skillet, sauté the onion and garlic. Add the shredded chicken and corn.
3. Stir in the cream cheese until it melts into a creamy sauce. Transfer to a small baking dish.
4. Top with shredded mozzarella.
5. Bake for 15-20 mins until hot and bubbly.

Ingredients

- Chicken Breast, cooked & shredded: 200g / 7 oz
- Cream Cheese: 60g / 2 oz
- Canned Corn, drained: 1/4 cup
- Mozzarella Cheese, shredded: 40g / 1.5 oz
- Onion & Garlic, chopped.

Macros

~530 kcal | P: 45g | F: 36g | C: 9g

POLISH KOTLET SCHABOWY (TURKEY VERSION)

Method

1. Season the turkey cutlet with salt and pepper.
2. Dip the cutlet in the beaten egg, allowing excess to drip off.
3. Press firmly into the crushed pork rinds to ensure a thick, even coating.
4. Fry in hot lard/ghee for 3-4 minutes per side, until deep golden brown and cooked through.
5. Serve with pickles and sautéed cabbage (kapusta).

Ingredients

- Turkey Breast Cutlet, pounded thin: 200g / 7 oz
- Egg, beaten: 1
- Breading: Crushed Pork Rinds (1/2 cup).
- Lard or Ghee for frying.

Macros

~500 kcal | P: 48g | F: 32g | C: 7g

CAJUN BLACKENED CHICKEN

Method

1. Generously coat the chicken breast on all sides with the Cajun spice mix.
2. Heat a cast-iron skillet over high heat until it is extremely hot.
3. Add ghee to the skillet, then immediately place the chicken breast in the pan.
4. Sear for 3-5 minutes per side. The spices will char and blacken, creating a delicious crust. Do not overcrowd the pan.
5. Serve immediately, perhaps with a cooling yogurt-based dip or alongside sautéed collard greens.

Ingredients

- Chicken Breast, pounded to even thickness: 200g / 7 oz
- Cajun Spice Rub: Smoked Paprika, Cayenne Pepper, Garlic Powder, Onion Powder, Dried Thyme, Black Pepper, Salt.
- Ghee or Avocado Oil: 1 tbsp

Macros

~490 kcal | P: 48g | F: 30g | C: 5g

TURKISH CHICKEN KEBAB (SHISH)

Method

1. Combine all marinade ingredients. Coat the chicken cubes thoroughly and marinate for at least 1 hour.
2. Thread the chicken onto skewers.
3. Grill or pan-sear the kebabs for 10-15 mins, turning occasionally, until cooked through and nicely charred.
4. Serve with a simple salad of tomato, cucumber, and onion, and a dollop of garlic yogurt.

Ingredients

- Chicken Breast, cut into large cubes: 220g / 8 oz
- Marinade: Greek Yogurt (3 tbsp); Tomato Paste (1 tbsp); Olive Oil; Paprika; Cumin; Garlic.

Macros

~490 kcal | P: 48g | F: 30g | C: 9g

RED MEAT:
BEEF, LAMB & PORK

This chapter is dedicated to the richest, most decadent flavors in the culinary world. Red meat, when chosen and prepared correctly, is an unparalleled source of high-quality protein, iron, and essential nutrients. We've reimagined global classics, stripping away heavy carbs and sugars to deliver pure, powerful, and deeply satisfying meals that will fuel your body and delight your senses.

KOREAN BULGOGI (BEEF)

Method

1. Marinate the thinly sliced beef for at least 30 minutes.
2. Heat a cast-iron skillet or grill pan over high heat.
3. Cook the meat in small batches for 1-2 mins per side until caramelized and cooked through. Don't overcrowd the pan.
4. Garnish with sliced green onion and sesame seeds. Serve with kimchi or a crisp lettuce salad.

Ingredients

- Beef Sirloin or Ribeye, very thinly sliced: 200g / 7 oz
- Marinade: Soy Sauce (3 tbsp); Sesame Oil (1 tbsp); minced Garlic; Swerve/Erythritol (1 tsp).
- Avocado Oil: 1 tsp
- Green onions and sesame seeds for garnish.

Macros

~530 kcal | P: 42g | F: 38g | C: 8g

HIGH-PROTEIN COWBOY CHILI (BEEF)

Method

1. In a pot, cook bacon until crisp. Remove bacon, leave fat.
2. Brown the beef cubes in the bacon fat. Add the onion and pepper, and cook until they are soft.
3. Add garlic and spices, cook for 1 min. Stir in tomatoes and 1 cup of water/broth.
4. Return bacon to the pot. Simmer on low for 1.5 to 2 hours, until the beef is tender and falling apart.
5. Serve in a bowl, topped with Greek yogurt or shredded cheddar.

Ingredients

- Beef Chuck, cubed: 200g / 7 oz
- Bacon, diced: 30g / 1 oz
- Onion, Bell Pepper, Garlic, chopped.
- Diced Tomatoes: 1/2 cup
- Spices: Chili powder, cumin, smoked paprika, oregano.

Macros

~560 kcal | P: 45g | F: 35g | C: 15g

GREEK SLOW-ROASTED LAMB (ARNI PSITO)

Method

1. Preheat oven to 325°F (160°C).
2. Make small incisions all over the lamb and stuff them with garlic slivers.
3. Rub the lamb with olive oil, lemon juice, oregano, salt, and pepper.
4. Place in a small baking dish, add a splash of water, and cover tightly with foil.
5. Roast for 2-3 hours until the meat is exceptionally tender. Serve with green beans.

Ingredients

- Lamb Shoulder or Leg: 250g / 8.8 oz
- Garlic: 4-5 cloves, slivered
- Lemon: 1/2, juiced
- Olive Oil: 1 tbsp
- Dried Oregano, Salt, Pepper.

Macros

~580 kcal | P: 45g | F: 42g | C: 7g

ITALIAN MEATBALLS IN MARINARA SAUCE

Method

1. In a bowl, gently mix the ground beef with Parmesan, egg, garlic, and parsley. Form into 3-4 large meatballs.
2. Brown the meatballs on all sides in an oiled skillet.
3. Pour over the marinara sauce, reduce the heat to low, cover, and simmer for 20-30 mins.
4. Top with mozzarella in the last 5 mins to melt. Serve over zucchini noodles.

Ingredients

- Ground Beef (80/20): 220g / 8 oz
- Parmesan Cheese, grated: 2 tbsp
- Egg: 1
- Garlic, minced; Parsley, chopped.
- Marinara Sauce (low-sugar): 1/2 cup
- Mozzarella Cheese (optional).

Macros

~540 kcal | P: 42g | F: 38g | C: 12g

HUNGARIAN GOULASH (BEEF)

Method

1. In a pot, brown the beef cubes in hot ghee. Remove and set aside.
2. Sauté the onion until soft and golden. Remove from heat and stir in the paprika and caraway seeds.
3. Return beef to the pot. Add tomato paste and broth.
4. Bring to a simmer, then cover and cook on low for 2-3 hours until the meat is fall-apart tender. Serve with cauliflower mash.

Ingredients

- Beef Chuck, cubed: 250g / 8.8 oz
- Onion, chopped: 1 large
- Spices: Sweet Paprika (2 tbsp); Caraway Seeds (1 tsp).
- Tomato Paste: 1 tbsp
- Beef Broth: 1 cup
- Ghee or Lard: 1 tbsp

Macros

~550 kcal | P: 48g | F: 35g | C: 13g

MOROCCAN LAMB TAGINE

Method

1. In a pot or skillet, brown the lamb. Add onion and cook until soft.
2. Add garlic and all spices, cook for 1 min until fragrant.
3. Pour in the broth and bring to a simmer. Cover and cook on low for 1.5 to 2 hours, or until the lamb is tender and falling apart.
4. Stir in olives and preserved lemon during the last 10 mins of cooking.

Ingredients

- Lamb Shoulder, cubed: 220g / 8 oz
- Onion, chopped; Garlic, minced.
- Spices: Turmeric, ginger, cumin, cinnamon.
- Chicken Broth: 1/2 cup
- Green Olives & Preserved Lemon (optional).

Macros

~570 kcal | P: 45g | F: 40g | C: 14g

TURKISH ADANA KEBAB (LAMB)

Method

1. In a bowl, combine ground lamb with the minced pepper, grated onion, and spices. Knead the mixture with your hands for several minutes until it becomes sticky.
2. Divide the mixture into two and mold it onto large, flat metal skewers.
3. Grill over charcoal or broil in the oven on high heat for 8-12 mins, turning occasionally, until cooked through and charred.
4. Serve with a yogurt-garlic sauce and a grilled tomato.

Ingredients

- Ground Lamb: 220g / 8 oz
- Red Bell Pepper, very finely minced: 1/4
- Onion, grated and squeezed dry: 1/4
- Spices: Red pepper flakes (Aleppo or Urfa), cumin, salt.

Macros

~540 kcal | P: 40g | F: 40g | C: 6g

GERMAN PORK SCHNITZEL

Method

1. Season the pork cutlet with salt and pepper.
2. Dip in egg, then press firmly into the pork rind/almond flour mixture to create a thick crust.
3. Shallow-fry in hot lard for 3-4 minutes per side, until deep golden brown and crispy.
4. Serve immediately with a lemon wedge and braised red cabbage.

Ingredients

- Pork Loin Cutlet, pounded very thin: 200g / 7 oz
- Egg, beaten: 1
- Breading: Crushed Pork Rinds (1/2 cup); Almond Flour (2 tbsp).
- Lard or Ghee for frying.

Macros

~520 kcal | P: 45g | F: 35g | C: 8g

NEW ZEALAND HERB-CRUSTED LAMB

Method

1. Preheat oven to 400°F (200°C). Season the lamb rack with salt and pepper, and sear it in a hot skillet on all sides.
2. Brush the fatty side of the lamb with Dijon mustard.
3. In a small bowl, mix all crust ingredients. Press this mixture firmly onto the mustard-coated side of the lamb.
4. Roast for 15-20 mins for medium-rare. Let it rest for 10 mins before slicing.

Ingredients

- Rack of Lamb, 2-3 ribs: ~250g / 8.8 oz
- Crust: Fresh Parsley & Mint (1/4 cup); Garlic (2 cloves); Almond Flour (2 tbsp); Olive Oil (1 tbsp).
- Dijon Mustard: 1 tbsp

Macros

~600 kcal | P: 45g | F: 45g | C: 6g

MEXICAN CARNE ASADA

Method

1. Marinate the steak for at least 1 hour (up to 4 hours).
2. Heat a grill or cast-iron skillet to very high heat.
3. Cook the steak for 3-5 mins per side for medium-rare.
4. Let the steak rest for 10 mins.
5. Slice thinly against the grain. Serve with fresh salsa, guacamole, and grilled onions.

Ingredients

- Flank or Skirt Steak: 200g / 7 oz
- Marinade: Lime Juice (1/4 cup); minced Garlic; chopped Cilantro; Cumin; pinch of chili powder.
- Avocado Oil: 1 tbsp

Macros

~510 kcal | P: 42g | F: 35g | C: 5g

CHINESE SWEET & SOUR PORK
(LOW-CARB)

Method

1. In a hot wok, stir-fry the pork in oil until it is browned. Add onion and pepper, cook until tender-crisp.
2. In a small bowl, whisk all sauce ingredients.
3. Pour the sauce into the wok. Stir continuously for 2-3 mins until the sauce thickens and glazes everything.
4. Serve immediately.

Ingredients

- Pork Tenderloin, cubed: 200g / 7 oz
- Bell Pepper & Onion, chopped.
- Sauce: Rice Vinegar (3 tbsp); Soy Sauce (2 tbsp); Swerve/Erythritol (1 tbsp); Tomato Paste (1 tsp).
- Avocado Oil for frying.

Macros

~540 kcal | P: 40g | F: 35g | C: 15g

LEBANESE KIBBEH
(BAKED, LOW-CARB)

Method

1. Preheat oven to 400°F (200°C).
2. In a bowl, thoroughly mix the ground meat, onion, almond flour, and all spices. Knead it well.
3. Press the mixture into a small, oiled baking dish. Score the top in a diamond pattern.
4. Bake for 25-30 mins until browned and cooked through.
5. Garnish with toasted pine nuts and serve with a dollop of Greek yogurt.

Ingredients

- Ground Lamb or Beef: 220g / 8 oz
- Onion, finely chopped: 1/2
- Almond Flour: 3 tbsp
- Spices: Allspice, cinnamon, cumin, salt, pepper.
- Pine Nuts, toasted (optional garnish).

Macros

~550 kcal | P: 42g | F: 38g | C: 10g

PERSIAN KOOBIDEH KEBAB (BEEF)

Method

1. In a bowl, combine ground beef, dried grated onion, and spices. Knead with your hands for 5-10 minutes until the mixture is very sticky and emulsified.
2. Divide the mixture and mold it onto large, flat metal skewers.
3. Grill over charcoal or broil on high heat for 8-12 minutes, turning occasionally, until the meat is cooked through.
4. Serve with a grilled tomato and a sprinkle of sumac.

Ingredients

- Ground Beef (80/20): 220g / 8 oz
- Onion, grated and squeezed dehydrated: 1/2
- Spices: Turmeric, sumac, salt, pepper.

Macros

~530 kcal | P: 40g | F: 38g | C: 7g

AMERICAN BEEF STIR-FRY

Method

1. In a hot wok, sear the beef slices in oil for 1-2 mins until just browned. Remove from the wok.
2. Add broccoli to the wok with a splash of water, cover, and steam for 2-3 mins.
3. Return beef to the wok. Add the sauce ingredients and stir-fry for 1-2 mins until everything is coated.
4. Serve immediately.

Ingredients

- Flank Steak, thinly sliced: 200g / 7 oz
- Broccoli Florets: 1.5 cups
- Sauce: Coconut Aminos or Soy Sauce (3 tbsp); minced Garlic; grated Ginger.
- Avocado Oil: 1 tbsp

Macros

~500 kcal | P: 42g | F: 32g | C: 12g

FRENCH CASSOULET (QUICK SKILLET VERSION)

Method

1. In a skillet, brown the sausage. Add onion and garlic, cook until soft.
2. Add the shredded duck/chicken, beans, tomatoes, and thyme.
3. Simmer for 15-20 minutes until the flavors have melded and the sauce has thickened.
4. (Optional) Top with crushed pork rinds and broil for 2 mins for a crispy crust.

Ingredients

- Pork Sausage (low-carb, e.g., Italian): 150g / 5.3 oz
- Duck Confit Leg or Chicken Thigh: 1, shredded (~100g)
- Canned White Beans (e.g., Cannellini), rinsed: 1/2 cup
- Diced Tomatoes: 1/2 cup
- Onion, Garlic, Thyme.

Macros

~580 kcal | P: 48g | F: 40g | C: 15g

SWEDISH MEATBALLS

Method

1. Gently mix ground meat with spices, salt, and pepper. Form into small meatballs.
2. Brown the meatballs on all sides in a hot skillet with butter. Remove meatballs.
3. Pour beef broth into the same skillet to deglaze. Stir in the heavy cream and simmer until the sauce thickens slightly.
4. Return meatballs to the pan and simmer in the sauce for 5-10 mins. Serve over cauliflower mash.

Ingredients

- Ground Beef/Pork Mix: 220g / 8 oz
- Sauce: Beef Broth (1/2 cup); Heavy Cream (1/4 cup).
- Spices for meatballs: Allspice, nutmeg.
- Butter/Ghee: 1 tbsp

Macros

~560 kcal | P: 42g | F: 40g | C: 9g

SHEPHERD'S PIE WITH CAULIFLOWER TOP

Method

1. Steam cauliflower until very tender, then blend with cream, Parmesan, salt, and pepper until smooth.
2. In a skillet, brown the ground lamb. Add diced vegetables and cook until tender. Stir in tomato paste and a splash of beef broth. Simmer for 10 mins.
3. Place the meat filling in a small baking dish. Spread the cauliflower mash evenly on top.
4. Bake at 400°F (200°C) for 20 minutes, then broil for 2-3 minutes, or until the top is golden.

Ingredients

- Ground Lamb: 200g / 7 oz
- Filling: Onion, Carrot, Celery (finely diced); Tomato Paste (1 tbsp).
- Topping: Cauliflower Florets (2 cups); Heavy Cream (2 tbsp); Parmesan cheese (2 tbsp).

Macros

~570 kcal | P: 45g | F: 38g | C: 15g

PAN-SEARED STEAK WITH GARLIC BUTTER

Method

1. Pat the steak very dry and season generously with salt and pepper.
2. Heat oil in a cast-iron skillet over high heat until smoking. Sear steak for 3-4 mins per side for medium-rare.
3. Lower the heat, add butter, garlic, and herbs to the pan.
4. As the butter melts, tilt the pan and use a spoon to baste the steak with the foaming butter for 1 minute.
5. Rest the steak for 10 mins before slicing.

Ingredients

- Ribeye or Sirloin Steak: 220g / 8 oz
- Butter: 2 tbsp
- Garlic: 3 cloves, smashed
- Fresh Rosemary or Thyme sprig.
- Avocado Oil: 1 tsp

Macros

~600 kcal | P: 42g | F: 48g | C: 2g

LONDON BROIL (FLANK STEAK)

Method

1. Marinate the steak for at least 1 hour (or up to 4 hours).
2. Heat a grill or skillet to very high heat.
3. Cook steak for 4-6 mins per side for medium-rare.
4. Let it rest for 10 mins.
5. Crucial: Slice the steak very thinly against the grain.

Ingredients

- Flank Steak: 220g / 8 oz
- Marinade: Olive Oil (2 tbsp); Balsamic Vinegar (1 tbsp); Soy Sauce (1 tbsp); minced Garlic.

Macros

~520 kcal | P: 45g | F: 36g | C: 4g

JAMAICAN JERK PORK

Method

1. Thoroughly coat the pork cubes in the Jerk marinade. Let it sit for at least 2 hours.
2. Slow Cooker: Cook on low for 4-6 hours.
3. Oven: Bake in a covered dish at 325°F (160°C) for 2-3 hours until tender.
4. Shred the pork with two forks. For a crispy finish, spread the shredded pork on a baking sheet and broil for 3-5 minutes, or until golden brown on all sides.

Ingredients

- Pork Shoulder, cubed: 220g / 8 oz
- Jerk Marinade: 2 tbsp of a sugar-free Jerk paste/marinade (contains scallions, habanero, thyme, allspice, etc.).

Macros

~550 kcal | P: 45g | F: 40g | C: 8g

VIETNAMESE LEMONGRASS PORK MEATBALLS

Method

1. In a bowl, combine all ingredients and mix well. Form into small meatballs.
2. Pan-fry the meatballs in a hot, oiled skillet, turning them, for 10-12 minutes until browned on all sides and cooked through.
3. Serve in lettuce cups with fresh mint and cucumber ribbons.

Ingredients

- Ground Pork: 220g / 8 oz
- Lemongrass, tough outer layers removed, finely minced: 1 tbsp
- Fish Sauce: 2 tsp
- Garlic, minced; Cilantro, chopped.

Macros

- **~530 kcal | P: 40g | F: 38g | C: 9g**

LOW-CARB BEEF BOURGUIGNON (FRENCH)

Method

1. In a bowl, combine all ingredients and mix well. Form into small meatballs.
2. Pan-fry the meatballs in a hot, oiled skillet, turning them, for 10-12 minutes until browned on all sides and cooked through.
3. Serve in lettuce cups with fresh mint and cucumber ribbons.

Ingredients

- Beef Chuck, cubed: 250g
- 8.8 oz Bacon, diced: 50g
- 1.8 oz Mushrooms, halved: 100g
- 3.5 oz Pearl Onions or one small onion, chopped: 50g
- 1.8 oz Garlic, minced: 2 cloves
- Dry Red Wine: 120ml
- 1/2 cup Beef Broth: 240ml
- 1 cup Tomato Paste: 1 tbsp
- Fresh Thyme;
- Bay Leaf Ghee: 1 tbsp

Macros

- **~560 kcal | P: 45g | F: 38g | C: 10g**

FISH & SEAFOOD

Welcome to the leanest, most nutrient-dense protein on the planet. Fish and seafood are rich in high-quality protein and essential omega-3 fatty acids, making them a cornerstone of a healthy diet. This chapter will take you on a global voyage, proving that fish can be fast, flavorful, and incredibly satisfying. From zesty ceviche to rich, fragrant curries, get ready to explore the ocean's bounty.

JAPANESE TERIYAKI SALMON

Method

1. Pat the salmon skin dry. Season with salt.
2. In a hot, non-stick skillet, sear the salmon, skin-side down, in oil for 4-5 minutes until crispy. Flip and cook for 2-3 mins more.
3. Lower the heat and pour in the sauce ingredients. Simmer for 1-2 mins as the sauce thickens and glazes the fish.
4. Serve with steamed asparagus or bok choy.

Ingredients

- Salmon Fillet, skin-on: 180g / 6.5 oz
- Sauce: Soy Sauce/Tamari (2 tbsp); Swerve/Erythritol (1 tsp); Sake/Mirin (1 tbsp); Grated Ginger.
- Avocado Oil: 1 tsp

Macros

~540 kcal | P: 38g | F: 40g | C: 8g

GREEK LEMON-HERB SALMON

Method

1. Preheat oven to 400°F (200°C).
2. Place salmon on a piece of parchment paper. Drizzle with olive oil and lemon juice. Top with garlic, oregano, and lemon slices.
3. Fold the parchment paper into a sealed packet (en papillote).
4. Bake for 15-18 mins, until the salmon is cooked through and flaky.
5. Open the packet carefully. Garnish with fresh herbs.

Ingredients

- Salmon Fillet: 180g / 6.5 oz
- Olive Oil: 1 tbsp
- Lemon: 1/2, juiced and sliced
- Garlic, minced: 2 cloves
- Dried Oregano: 1 tsp
- Fresh Dill & Parsley, chopped.

Macros

~510 kcal | P: 38g | F: 38g | C: 5g

PERUVIAN CEVICHE

Method

1. In a glass bowl, combine the fish, lime juice, and salt. Ensure the fish is fully submerged in juice.
2. Cover and refrigerate for 20-30 mins, until the fish becomes opaque and "cooked" by the acid.
3. Gently drain some of the excess lime juice.
4. Stir in the red onion, cilantro, and chili paste.
5. Just before serving, fold the avocado in. Serve in a chilled bowl.

Ingredients

- Firm White Fish (e.g., Sea Bass, Halibut), cubed: 200g / 7 oz
- Lime Juice, fresh squeezed: 1/2 cup
- Red Onion, thinly sliced: 1/4
- Cilantro, chopped: 1/4 cup
- Aji Amarillo Paste or minced Jalapeño: 1 tsp
- Avocado, cubed: 1/2

Macros

✔ **~380 kcal | P: 35g | F: 20g | C: 12g**

ITALIAN SHRIMP "PASTA"

Method

1. In a large skillet, heat butter and oil. Sauté garlic for 1 min. Add shrimp and red pepper flakes, cook for 2 mins until pink. Remove shrimp.
2. Add white wine to the pan to deglaze. Add cherry tomatoes and cook until they soften.
3. Add the zoodles to the pan and toss for 1-2 mins until just tender.
4. Return shrimp to the pan, toss with parsley, and serve immediately.

Ingredients

- Shrimp, peeled & deveined: 200g / 7 oz
- Zucchini Noodles ("Zoodles"): 1 large zucchini
- Cherry Tomatoes, halved: 1/2 cup
- Garlic, sliced: 3 cloves
- White Wine (dry): 1/4 cup
- Butter & Olive Oil: 1 tbsp each
- Red Pepper Flakes, Parsley.

Macros

✔ **~480 kcal | P: 38g | F: 30g | C: 14g**

MEXICAN FISH TACOS
(DECONSTRUCTED BOWL)

Method

1. Rub the fish with spices, salt, and pepper.
2. Pan-sear the fish in a hot, oiled skillet for 3-4 mins per side until cooked and flaky.
3. In a bowl, assemble a bed of lime-tossed cabbage slaw.
4. Flake the cooked fish over the slaw. Top with sliced avocado and a drizzle of the chipotle crema.

Ingredients

- Cod or Mahi-Mahi Fillet: 200g / 7 oz
- Spice Rub: Cumin, chili powder, paprika.
- Slaw: Shredded Cabbage; Lime Juice.
- Crema: Greek Yogurt (3 tbsp); Chipotle powder.
- Avocado, sliced: 1/2

Macros

✔ **~520 kcal | P: 40g | F: 32g | C: 15g**

INDIAN FISH CURRY
(GOAN-STYLE)

Method

1. In a skillet, sauté the onion in oil. Add ginger-garlic paste and spices, and cook for 1 minute.
2. Add the tomato and cook until it breaks down.
3. Stir in the coconut milk and bring to a gentle simmer.
4. Gently place the fish cubes into the curry. Cover and poach for 5-7 mins until the fish is cooked through. Garnish with fresh cilantro.

Ingredients

- Firm White Fish (e.g., Cod, Halibut), cubed: 200g / 7 oz
- Full-Fat Coconut Milk: 1/2 cup
- Onion, chopped; Ginger-Garlic paste.
- Spices: Turmeric, coriander, cumin, chili powder.
- Tomato, chopped: 1
- Coconut Oil: 1 tbsp

Macros

✔ **~530 kcal | P: 40g | F: 38g | C: 12g**

CHINESE SHRIMP & BROCCOLI STIR-FRY

Method

1. Blanch or steam broccoli for 2 mins until bright green and tender-crisp.
2. In a hot wok or skillet, heat avocado oil. Add shrimp and stir-fry for 1-2 mins until they start to turn pink.
3. Add the broccoli and the sauce ingredients to the wok.
4. Stir-fry for another 1-2 mins until everything is coated and the shrimp are fully cooked.

Ingredients

- Shrimp, peeled & deveined: 200g / 7 oz
- Broccoli Florets: 1.5 cups
- Sauce: Soy Sauce (2 tbsp); Sesame Oil (1 tsp); minced Garlic & Ginger.
- Avocado Oil: 1 tbsp

Macros

~450 kcal | P: 40g | F: 25g | C: 15g

BRAZILIAN MOQUECA (FISH STEW)

Method

1. In a pot, sauté the onion, pepper, and garlic in oil until tender.
2. Add the tomato and cook for 2 mins. Stir in the coconut milk.
3. Bring to a simmer. Gently add the fish to the stew.
4. Cook for 5-8 mins until the fish is opaque. Turn off the heat and stir in the lime juice and a large handful of fresh cilantro.

Ingredients

- Firm White Fish, cubed: 200g / 7 oz
- Full-Fat spoons of coconut Milk: 1/2 cup
- Belltablespoonper & Onion, sliced.
- Tomato, tablespoon: 1
- Dendê Oil (Palm Oil) or Olive Oil: 1 tbsp
- Garlic, Lime Juice, Cilantro.

Macros

~550 kcal | P: 40g | F: 40g | C: 13g

FRENCH BOUILLABAISSE (SIMPLE VERSION)

Method

1. In a pot, sauté the onion, leek, and fennel in olive oil until tender. Add garlic and tomato paste.
2. Deglaze with white wine. Add broth, saffron, and bay leaf. Simmer for 15 mins.
3. Add the firm fish first and cook for 3 minutes. Then add shrimp and mussels.
4. Cover and cook for an additional 3-5 minutes, until the shrimp are pink and the mussels have opened. Discard any unopened mussels.

Ingredients

- Mixed Seafood: 250g / 8.8 oz (e.g., firm fish, shrimp, mussels)
- Fish or Chicken Broth: 1.5 cups
- Onion, Leek, & Fennel, chopped.
- Aromatics: Saffron threads, bay leaf, tomato paste (1 tbsp).
- Dry White Wine: 1/4 cup

Macros

~540 kcal | P: 45g | F: 32g | C: 15g

SCANDINAVIAN GRAVLAX

Method

1. Combine the cure mix ingredients.
2. Lay half the dill on a plate. Place salmon on top. Cover the entire surface with the cured mix, then top with the remaining dill.
3. Wrap tightly in plastic wrap. Place in the fridge with a weight on top (e.g., a can of beans) for 24-48 hours, flipping once.
4. Unwrap, rinse off the cure, and pat dry. Slice thinly and serve with the yogurt-mustard sauce and a cucumber salad.

Ingredients

- Salmon Fillet, sashimi-grade, skin-off: 180g / 6.5 oz
- Cure Mix: Sea Salt (2 tablespoons), Swerve/Erythritol (1 tablespoon), and cracked black pepper (1 tablespoon).
- Fresh Dill, chopped: 1 large bunch
- Mustard Sauce: Dijon Mustard, Greek Yogurt, chopped dill.

Macros

~450 kcal | P: 35g | F: 32g | C: 3g

AMERICAN GRILLED SALMON

Method

1. Preheat grill to medium-high heat. Oil the grates.
2. Mix herb butter ingredients in a small bowl.
3. Brush salmon with olive oil, season with salt and pepper.
4. Grill salmon skin-side down for 6-8 mins, then flip and grill 3-4 mins more.
5. Top with herb butter and lemon slices. Serve with grilled asparagus.

Ingredients

- Salmon Fillet, skin-on: 180g / 6.5 oz
- Herb Butter: Butter (2 tbsp); minced Garlic (2 cloves);
- fresh Dill & Parsley (2 tbsp each)
- Lemon, sliced: 1/2
- Olive Oil: 1 tsp
- Asparagus spears: 6-8 (for serving)

Macros

~520 kcal | P: 38g | F: 38g | C: 4g

KOREAN SPICY TUNA

Method

1. Mix all sauce ingredients in a bowl.
2. Marinate tuna steaks in half the sauce for 15 mins.
3. Heat oil in a hot skillet. Sear tuna for 1-2 mins per side (keep center rare).
4. Slice tuna and serve over cucumber julienne. Drizzle with remaining sauce and sprinkle with sesame seeds.

Ingredients

- Tuna Steaks (sashimi-grade): 200g / 7 oz
- Korean Sauce: Gochujang (2 tbsp)
- Soy Sauce (1 tbsp)
- Sesame Oil (1 tsp)
- Rice Vinegar (1 tbsp); minced Garlic & Ginger
- Cucumber, julienned: 1/2
- Sesame Seeds: 1 tbsp
- Avocado Oil: 1 tsp

Macros

~480 kcal | P: 40g | F: 28g | C: 12g

MOROCCAN FISH TAGINE

Method

1. Heat oil in a tagine or heavy skillet. Sauté the onion until soft.
2. Add spice mix, cook for 1 min until fragrant.
3. Add tomato, cook until it breaks down (5 mins).
4. Gently nestle fish cubes into the sauce. Add olives and preserved lemon.
5. Cover and simmer for 8-10 mins until fish is cooked through. Garnish with cilantro.

Ingredients

- Firm White Fish (Cod/Halibut), cubed: 200g / 7 oz
- Moroccan Spice Mix: Cumin, Coriander, Turmeric, Cinnamon, Ginger
- Onion, sliced: 1/2
- Tomato, chopped: 1 medium
- Green Olives, pitted: 1/4 cup
- Preserved Lemon, chopped: 1 tsp (optional)
- Olive Oil: 1 tbsp

Macros

✔ **~510 kcal | P: 38g | F: 32g | C: 14g**

LEBANESE SAMAK MESHWI (GRILLED FISH)

Method

1. Score fish skin in diagonal cuts. Marinate for 30 mins.
2. Preheat grill to medium-high. Grill the fish for 6-8 minutes per side, until charred and cooked through.
3. Mix tahini sauce ingredients until smooth.
4. Serve grilled fish with tahini sauce and fresh tomato-cucumber salad.

Ingredients

- Whole Fish (Sea Bass/Snapper) or thick fillets: 220g / 8 oz
- Marinade: Olive Oil (3 tbsp);
- Lemon Juice (2 tbsp); minced Garlic (3 cloves); Sumac (1 tsp); dried Oregano
- Tahini Sauce: Tahini (2 tbsp); Lemon Juice;
- Water to thin; minced Garlic
- Tomato & Cucumber salad for serving

Macros

✔ **~490 kcal | P: 36g | F: 35g | C: 8g**

RUSSIAN FISH UNDER MARINADE

Method

1. Pan-fry seasoned fish fillets in oil until golden and cooked through. Set aside.
2. In the same pan, sauté onions and carrots until soft (8-10 mins).
3. Add vinegar, bay leaves, salt, and pepper. Simmer for 5 mins.
4. Pour hot marinade over the fish. Cool to room temperature, then refrigerate for at least 2 hours.
5. Serve cold, topped with sour cream and fresh dill.

Ingredients

- White Fish Fillets (Cod/Haddock): 200g / 7 oz
- Marinade: Onion, thinly sliced (1 large); Carrots, julienned (1 medium); White Vinegar (3 tbsp); Olive Oil (2 tbsp)
- Bay Leaves: 2
- Sour Cream: 3 tbsp
- Fresh Dill, chopped

Macros

~530 kcal | P: 35g | F: 38g | C: 12g

VIETNAMESE CHA CA (TURMERIC FISH)

Method

1. Marinate fish cubes for 20 mins.
2. Heat oil in a skillet. Cook fish until golden and cooked through (6-8 mins).
3. Add dill and green onions to the pan, toss for 1 min until wilted.
4. 4Serve immediately, garnished with crushed peanuts and lime wedges.

Ingredients

- Firm White Fish, cubed: 200g / 7 oz
- •Marinade: Fish Sauce (2 tbsp); Turmeric (1 tsp); minced Garlic & Ginger; Lime Juice
- Fresh Dill, chopped: 1/2 cup
- Green Onions, chopped: 1/4 cup
- Peanuts, crushed: 2 tbsp
- Avocado Oil: 1 tbsp

Macros

~500 kcal | P: 38g | F: 32g | C: 13g

TURKISH BALIK
(HERB-CRUSTED FISH)

Method

1. Preheat oven to 400°F (200°C).
2. In a food processor, pulse herbs, garlic, and walnuts. Drizzle in olive oil to make a paste.
3. Place fish on a baking sheet. Spread the herb mixture on top.
4. Arrange lemon and tomato slices around the fish.
5. Bake for 15-18 mins until fish flakes easily and crust is golden.

Ingredients

- Sea Bass or Salmon Fillet: 180g / 6.5 oz
- Herb Crust: Fresh Parsley (1/2 cup); fresh Dill (1/4 cup); Garlic (2 cloves); Walnuts (2 tbsp); Olive Oil (2 tbsp)
- Lemon, sliced: 1/2
- Tomato, sliced: 1 medium

Macros

~480 kcal | P: 36g | F: 32g | C: 9g

PORTUGUESE BACALHAU
(SALT COD)

Method

1. If using salt cod, soak overnight and flake. If using fresh cod, season it generously with salt and let it sit for 30 minutes, then flake it.
2. Boil potato cubes until tender (8-10 mins). Drain.
3. Heat olive oil, sauté onion and garlic until golden.
4. Add flaked cod and potatoes, gently mix and heat through (5 mins).
5. Stir in olives, chopped egg, and parsley. Serve warm.

Ingredients

- Salt Cod, soaked & flaked: 200g / 7 oz (or use fresh cod with extra salt)
- Potatoes, cubed small: 100g / 3.5 oz
- Portuguese Sofrito: Onion, chopped (1 medium); Garlic (3 cloves); Olive Oil (3 tbsp)
- Black Olives, pitted: 1/4 cup
- Hard-Boiled Egg, chopped: 1
- Fresh Parsley, chopped

Macros

~520 kcal | P: 42g | F: 30g | C: 11g

PLANT PROTEINS

Welcome to the ultimate plant-based protein challenge. Achieving 32+ grams of protein from plants alone requires a strategic approach, creativity, and a willingness to explore protein-dense combinations. These recipes demonstrate that plant-based eating can be both satisfying and incredibly protein-rich, utilizing legumes, seeds, nuts, tofu, and plant-based protein powders to provide the amino acids your body needs.

INDIAN TRIPLE-DAL PROTEIN BOWL

Method

1. Rinse and cook the dal mix in 3 cups of water with turmeric until soft and creamy (approximately 25-30 minutes).
2. In a separate pan, heat coconut oil. Add onion, cook until golden. Add ginger-garlic paste and spices, and cook for 1 minute.
3. Add diced tomato, cook until soft. Stir this mixture into the cooked dal.
4. Add chopped spinach and simmer for 5 mins. Remove from heat.
5. Key Step: Stir in the protein powder gradually while the dal is still warm (not boiling) to prevent clumping.
6. Serve hot, garnished with fresh cilantro.

Ingredients

- Triple Dal Mix: Red Lentils (40g dry); Yellow Split Peas (40g dry); Black Lentils/Urad Dal (30g dry)
- Unflavored Plant Protein Powder: 15g / 0.5 oz
- Coconut Oil: 1 tbsp
- Spices: Turmeric, cumin, coriander, garam masala, ginger-garlic paste
- Onion, chopped; Tomato, diced
- Spinach, chopped: 1 cup

Macros

~580 kcal | P: 35g | F: 18g | C: 65g

MEDITERRANEAN POWER FALAFEL BOWL

Method

1. In a food processor, pulse chickpeas until roughly chopped (not smooth). Add garlic, parsley, cumin, coriander, and protein powder. Pulse to combine.
2. Add 2 tbsp tahini and lemon juice. Mix until the mixture holds together but is not too sticky or mushy.
3. Form into 6-8 small falafel balls. Pan-fry in olive oil for 3-4 mins per side until golden and crispy.
4. Prepare a fresh salad with cucumber, tomato, and red onion.
5. Assembly: Serve falafel over the salad. Drizzle with remaining tahini thinned with lemon juice and water. Sprinkle hemp seeds on top.

Ingredients

- Canned Chickpeas, drained & rinsed: 240g / 8.5 oz
- Tahini (Sesame Seed Paste): 3 tbsp
- Hemp Seeds: 2 tbsp
- Unflavored Plant Protein Powder: 15g / 0.5 oz
- Falafel Spices: Cumin, coriander, parsley, garlic, lemon juice
- Olive Oil: 1 tbsp
- Salad: Cucumber, tomato, red onion, parsley

Macros

~520 kcal | P: 42g | F: 30g | C: 11g

ASIAN DOUBLE-SOY PROTEIN STIR-FRY

Method

1. Press the tofu to remove excess water, then cube it into small pieces. Crumble tempeh into bite-sized pieces.
2. In a hot wok or large skillet, heat sesame oil. Add tofu and tempeh, stir-fry for 5-7 mins until golden and crispy.
3. Add broccoli and bell pepper, stir-fry for 3-4 mins until tender-crisp.
4. Add edamame and stir-fry for 2 mins.
5. In a small bowl, whisk all sauce ingredients. Pour over the stir-fry and toss to coat.
6. Garnish with sesame seeds and serve immediately.

Ingredients

- Extra-Firm Tofu, cubed: 150g / 5.3 oz
- Tempeh, crumbled: 80g / 2.8 oz
- Edamame, shelled: 80g / 2.8 oz
- Sauce: Almond Butter (2 tbsp); Soy Sauce/Tamari (2 tbsp); Rice Vinegar (1 tbsp); Sriracha; minced Ginger & Garlic
- Broccoli & Bell Pepper, chopped
- Sesame Oil: 1 tbsp
- Sesame Seeds for garnish

Macros

✔ **~590 kcal | P: 38g | F: 35g | C: 35g**

MEXICAN BLACK BEAN POWER BOWL

Method

1. In a pot, heat olive oil. Add black beans with their liquid and all spices. Simmer for 10 mins until thick and flavorful.
2. Key Step: Remove from heat and gradually stir in the unflavored protein powder, mixing well to prevent clumping.
3. In a bowl, layer the cooked quinoa as the base.
4. Top with the protein-enhanced black beans.
5. Add sliced avocado and sprinkle generously with the mixed seeds (pumpkin, sunflower, and chia).
6. Finish with fresh cilantro and a squeeze of lime juice.

Ingredients

- Canned Black Beans, rinsed: 240g / 8.5 oz
- Cooked Quinoa: 100g / 3.5 oz (about 1/2 cup cooked)
- Unflavored Plant Protein Powder: 15g / 0.5 oz
- Protein Seeds Mix: Pumpkin Seeds (3 tbsp); Sunflower Seeds (1 tbsp); Chia Seeds (2 tbsp)
- Avocado: 1/2, sliced
- Spices: Cumin, chili powder, smoked paprika, garlic powder
- Lime juice, cilantro
- Olive Oil: 1 tbsp

Macros

✔ **~620 kcal | P: 32g | F: 27g | C: 72g**

LOW-CARB INDIAN CURRIES

Experience the soul of Indian cuisine, reimagined for a high-protein world. This chapter delivers the rich, aromatic curries you crave, without the carbs that hold you back. From tender Chicken Tikka to rich Lamb Rogan Josh, each recipe is a flavor-packed powerhouse designed to fuel your body and delight your senses.

LOW-CARB CHICKEN TIKKA MASALA

Method

1. Marinate chicken for 30+ mins. Grill or pan-sear until cooked.
2. Sauté the onion in ghee. Add spices, cook 1 min. Add tomatoes, simmer 10 mins.
3. Stir in cream, then add cooked chicken. Simmer 5 mins.
4. Serve with cauliflower rice.

Ingredients

Chicken Marinade:

- Chicken Breast, cubed: 250g / 8.8 oz
- Greek Yogurt: 2 tbsp
- Spices: Garam masala, turmeric, ginger-garlic paste, lemon juice.

Sauce:

- Crushed Tomatoes: 200g / 7 oz
- Onion, garlic, and ginger, chopped.
- Heavy Cream: 3 tbsp
- Spices: Garam masala, cumin, coriander, paprika.
- Ghee/Oil: 1 tbsp

Macros

~550 kcal | P: 50g | F: 35g | C: 12g

LAMB ROGAN JOSH

Method

1. Brown the lamb in ghee, then set it aside.
2. Sauté the onion until golden. Add spices, cook 1 min.
3. Return lamb to the pot. Slowly stir in whisked yogurt. Add 1 cup of water.
4. Cover and simmer on low heat for 1.5 to 2 hours, or until the meat is tender and falling apart.
5. Serve with steamed green beans.

Ingredients

- Lamb Shoulder, cubed: 250g / 8.8 oz
- Greek Yogurt: 100g / 3.5 oz
- Onion, chopped; ginger-garlic paste.
- Spices: Kashmiri chili, fennel, cardamom, cloves, cinnamon.
- Ghee/Oil: 1 tbsp

Macros

~580 kcal | P: 48g | F: 40g | C: 10g

PANEER BUTTER MASALA (VEG)

Method

1. Sauté onion, garlic, tomatoes, and cashews for 10 mins until soft. Cool, then blend into a smooth paste.
2. Strain paste into the pan. Add butter & spices. Simmer 10 mins.
3. Stir in cream and fenugreek. Add paneer, cook 5 mins.
4. Serve with a cucumber salad.

Ingredients

- Paneer, cubed: 200g / 7 oz
- Tomatoes: 2, chopped
- Raw Cashews: 30g / 1 oz
- Onion, chopped; ginger-garlic paste.
- Heavy Cream: 3 tbsp
- Spices: Garam masala, dried fenugreek (kasoori methi).
- Butter/Ghee: 1 tbsp

Macros

~540 kcal | P: 35g | F: 42g | C: 15g

"KETO" DAL MAKHANI (LENTIL-FREE)

Method

1. Roast eggplant until completely soft. Scoop out flesh and mash.
2. Sauté the onion in butter. Add spices, cook 1 min. Add tomato puree and simmer for 10 minutes.
3. Stir in mashed eggplant and black soybeans. Simmer 10 mins.
4. Stir in the cream and cook for an additional 5 minutes.
5. Serve on its own or with cauliflower rice.

Ingredients

- Canned Black Soybeans, rinsed: 100g / 3.5 oz
- Small Eggplant: 1
- Tomato Puree: 150g / 5.3 oz
- Onion, chopped; ginger-garlic paste.
- Heavy Cream: 3 tbsp
- Butter/Ghee: 1 tbsp
- Spices: Garam masala, cumin, smoked paprika.

Macros

~490 kcal | P: 35g | F: 35g | C: 18g

HIGH-PROTEIN SALADS

WITH YOGURT-BASED DRESSING

In this chapter, we'll prove that a salad is not just an appetizer but a complete, satisfying meal that can provide your required protein intake. The secret is simple: we use protein-rich bases and replace high-calorie mayonnaise and oil-based dressings with a light, creamy, and protein-packed sauce made from Greek yogurt.

WHAT CAN I USE INSTEAD OF GREEK YOGURT?

Greek yogurt is the star of our dressings, thanks to its creamy texture, tangy flavor, and high protein content. However, if you need a substitute due to dietary restrictions or simply don't have it on hand, here are some excellent alternatives.

Please note That Swapping out the Greek yogurt will alter the final nutritional values of the recipe, particularly the total protein count. The macros provided for each recipe are calculated using Greek yogurt.

OPTION 1: TO KEEP IT CREAMY AND HIGH-PROTEIN

Low-Fat Cottage Cheese (or Quark): This is the best substitute for maximizing protein.

1. How to use: Blend it with a splash of water, milk, or lemon juice until smooth and yogurt-like.
2. Pros: Very high in protein, often even more than Greek yogurt.

Sour Cream (Light): A classic alternative that provides excellent creaminess.

1. Usage: Use as a direct 1:1 replacement.
2. Pros: Delivers a rich, creamy texture and familiar taste.

OPTION 2: FOR DAIRY-FREE AND VEGAN DIETS

Unsweetened Coconut Yogurt: The best dairy-free option for a creamy texture.

1. How to use: Use it just like Greek yogurt. Choose a thick, plain variety.
2. Pros: Excellent creamy texture, completely dairy-free

Mashed Avocado: A surprisingly effective and healthy alternative.

1. How to use: Mash a ripe avocado with a fork and add lemon juice (to prevent browning), salt, and spices.
2. Pros: Provides healthy fats and a creamy texture.

Silken Tofu: The perfect base for a vegan cream sauce.

1. How to use: Blend it with lemon juice, spices, and a touch of soy sauce until smooth.
2. Pros: Neutral flavor, great creamy texture, contains plant-based protein, and is dairy-free.

"GREEK ISLAND" CHICKEN SALAD

Method

1. Season the chicken with salt, pepper, and oregano, then grill or bake it until cooked through and dice it.
2. Roughly chop the vegetables. Cube the feta cheese.
3. For the dressing, whisk together yogurt, minced garlic, and chopped dill.
4. Combine all ingredients and toss with the dressing.

Ingredients

- Chicken breast (180g / 6.5 oz)
- one cucumber, one tomato
- 1/2 bell pepper
- 1/4 red onion
- feta cheese (30g / 1 oz)
- 2% Greek yogurt (100g / 3.5 oz)
- one garlic clove, dill, oregano, salt, pepper

Macros

~480 kcal | Protein: 45g | Fat: 22g | Carbs: 15g

"COBB LITE" TURKEY SALAD

Method

1. Dice the cooked turkey and eggs. Slice the avocado and tomatoes.
2. For the dressing, mix the yogurt and mustard.
3. Arrange the turkey, eggs, avocado, and tomatoes on a bed of romaine lettuce. Drizzle with the dressing.

Ingredients

- Turkey breast (150g / 5.3 oz),
- two hard-boiled eggs, 1/2 avocado,
- 5-6 cherry tomatoes,
- romaine lettuce,
- 2% Greek yogurt (80g / 2.8 oz),
- 1 tsp Dijon mustard.

Macros

~520 kcal | Protein: 48g | Fat: 30g | Carbs: 12g

TUNA AND WHITE BEAN SALAD

Method

1. Drain the tuna and rinse the beans. Finely chop the celery, onion, and parsley.
2. Mix the yogurt with the mustard.
3. Combine all ingredients and gently mix.

Ingredients

- Canned tuna in water (1 can, ~130g / 4.5 oz, drained),
- canned white beans (150g / 5.3 oz),
- one celery stalk, 1/4 red onion,
- 2% Greek yogurt (80g / 2.8 oz),
- 1 tsp whole-grain mustard, parsley.

Macros

~450 kcal | Protein: 42g | Fat: 10g | Carbs: 35g

SPICY SHRIMP AND MANGO SALAD

Method

1. Sauté the shrimp with minced garlic for 2-3 minutes.
2. Dice the mango and bell pepper.
3. For the dressing, mix the yogurt, curry powder, and lime juice.
4. Combine the cooled shrimp, mango, bell pepper, and fresh cilantro. Toss with the dressing.

Ingredients

- Shrimp, peeled (150g / 5.3 oz),
- 1/2 firm mango,
- 1/2 bell pepper,
- 2% Greek yogurt (80g / 2.8 oz),
- 1/2 tsp curry powder, lime juice, cilantro, garlic.

Macros

~410 kcal | Protein: 35g | Fat: 12g | Carbs: 30g

"CAESAR 2.0" SALMON SALAD

Method

1. Grill or bake the salmon, then flake it into pieces. Hard-boil the eggs.
2. For the dressing, whisk together yogurt, grated garlic, and lemon juice.
3. Tear the romaine leaves, then top with salmon, eggs, and chickpeas. Drizzle with dressing and sprinkle with Parmesan.

Ingredients

- Salmon fillet (150g / 5.3 oz)
- romaine lettuce,
- four quail eggs,
- roasted chickpeas (30g / 1 oz),
- Parmesan cheese (15g / 0.5 oz),
- 2% Greek yogurt (80g / 2.8 oz), garlic, lemon juice.

Macros

~550 kcal | Protein: 42g | Fat: 32g | Carbs: 20g

WARM CHICKEN LIVER SALAD

Method

1. Sauté the chicken livers until cooked through. Sauté the chopped onion and carrot until soft.
2. Dice the livers and eggs.
3. Place the arugula on a plate, and top with the livers, eggs, and warm vegetables.
4. Drizzle with a yogurt-mustard dressing.

Ingredients

- Chicken livers (200g / 7 oz)
- two hard-boiled eggs
- one onion
- one carrot
- arugula (50g / 1.8 oz)
- 2% Greek yogurt (80g / 2.8 oz)
- 1 tsp Dijon mustard.

Macros

~490 kcal | Protein: 45g | Fat: 24g | Carbs: 20g

ASIAN-STYLE BEEF AND GINGER SALAD

Method

1. Quickly stir-fry thinly sliced beef. Julienne the carrot and cucumber.
2. For the dressing, mix the yogurt, soy sauce, grated ginger, minced garlic, and lime juice.
3. Combine the greens, vegetables, and beef. Toss with the dressing and sprinkle with sesame seeds.

Ingredients

- Beef steak (150g / 5.3 oz), mixed greens
- 1/2 carrot
- 1/2 cucumber
- 2% Greek yogurt (80g / 2.8 oz)
- 1 tbsp soy sauce
- fresh ginger (1-inch piece)
- garlic, lime juice, sesame seeds

Macros

✔ **~470 kcal | Protein: 42g | Fat: 25g | Carbs: 15g**

SMOKED CHICKEN AND GARLIC SALAD

Method

1. Dice the chicken, celery, and eggs into small pieces.
2. For the dressing, mix the yogurt with pressed garlic and chopped dill.
3. Combine all ingredients. Perfect for a quick meal prep.

Ingredients

- Smoked chicken breast (180g / 6.5 oz)
- two celery stalks
- two hard-boiled eggs
- 2% Greek yogurt (100g / 3.5 oz)
- two garlic cloves, and dill

Macros

✔ **~460 kcal | Protein: 44g | Fat: 25g | Carbs: 10g**

TOFU AND GINGER DRESSING BOWL (VEGETARIAN)

Method

1. Cube the tofu, marinate it in soy sauce, and bake until golden. Steam the broccoli.
2. For the dressing, whisk together yogurt, grated ginger, and lime juice.
3. Assemble the bowl with quinoa, tofu, broccoli, and edamame. Drizzle with the dressing.

Ingredients

- Extra-firm tofu (200g / 7 oz),
- cooked quinoa (100g / 3.5 oz),
- broccoli (100g / 3.5 oz),
- edamame (50g / 1.8 oz),
- 2% Greek yogurt (80g / 2.8 oz),
- soy sauce, fresh ginger, lime juice.

Macros

~480 kcal | Protein: 35g | Fat: 20g | Carbs: 40g

TURKEY MEATBALL SALAD

Method

1. Dice the chicken, celery, and eggs into small pieces.
2. For the dressing, mix the yogurt with pressed garlic and chopped dill.
3. Combine all ingredients. Perfect for a quick meal prep.

Ingredients

- Ground turkey (180g / 6.5 oz)
- canned chickpeas (80g / 2.8 oz)
- cherry tomatoes
- cucumber
- spinach
- 2% Greek yogurt (80g / 2.8 oz)
- parsley, lemon juice

Macros

~490 kcal | Protein: 43g | Fat: 22g | Carbs: 28g

WARMING HIGH-PROTEIN SOUPS

A soup is the perfect dish for lunch or dinner, capable of warming you up, satisfying your hunger, and providing your body with a necessary dose of protein. In this chapter, we move away from traditional light broths to create thick, hearty, and complete first courses, where every serving is a trustworthy source of energy.

CHICKEN SOUP WITH EGG RIBBONS AND HERBS

Method

1. Dice the chicken, carrot, and onion.
2. In boiling broth, cook the chicken and vegetables until tender (10-15 minutes). Add the green peas.
3. In a separate bowl, beat the eggs with a fork.
4. While stirring the soup to create a swirl, slowly pour in the beaten eggs in a thin stream. They will form delicate ribbons.
5. Remove from heat, add plenty of fresh herbs, and season with salt and pepper to taste.

Ingredients

- Chicken breast (200g / 7 oz)
- two eggs, chicken broth (400ml / 1.7 cups)
- 1/2 carrot
- 1/2 onion
- frozen green peas (50g / 1.8 oz)
- fresh dill, and parsley

Macros

✓ **~450 kcal | Protein: 45g | Fat: 20g | Carbs: 15g**

HEARTY TOMATO SOUP WITH BEEF MEATBALLS AND BEANS

Method

1. Form small meatballs from the ground beef.
2. In a pot, sauté the chopped onion, garlic, and bell pepper. Add the tomatoes and 200ml (0.8 cups) of water/broth, and bring to a boil.
3. Add the meatballs and spices to the soup and cook for 15 minutes.
4. Finally, add the rinsed beans and cook for an additional 5 minutes.

Ingredients

- Lean ground beef (150g / 5.3 oz), canned red kidney beans (100g / 3.5 oz), diced tomatoes (300g / 10.5 oz), onion, garlic, bell pepper, smoked paprika, oregano, basil.

Macros

✓ **~520 kcal | Protein: 42g | Fat: 25g | Carbs: 30g**

CREAMY LENTIL SOUP WITH SMOKED TURKEY

Method

1. Sauté the chopped vegetables in a pot. Add the rinsed lentils, spices, and 500ml (2.1 cups) of water. Cook for 20 minutes, or until the lentils are tender and fully cooked.
2. Blend the soup until smooth.
3. Dice the smoked turkey into small cubes.
4. Ladle the soup into bowls and top with a handful of diced turkey.

Ingredients

- Red lentils (100g / 3.5 oz), smoked turkey breast (150g / 5.3 oz), carrot, onion, celery root, turmeric, and cumin.

Macros

~480 kcal | P: 40g | F: 15g | C: 45g

FINNISH SALMON SOUP (LOHIKEITTO)

Method

1. Dice the potatoes and slice the leek. Add 400ml (1.7 cups) of water and cook until the potatoes are tender but still firm to the bite.
2. Cut the salmon into large cubes and add to the soup. Cook for 5-7 minutes (do not overcook the fish!).
3. Pour in the cream, add salt, pepper, and a generous amount of dill. Heat through without boiling.

Ingredients

- Skinless salmon fillet (200g / 7 oz), 1-2 potatoes, one leek (white part), 10-20% cream (100ml / 0.4 cups), plenty of fresh dill.

Macros

~550 kcal | P: 38g | F: 35g | C: 20g

SPICY MEXICAN CHICKEN SOUP WITH CORN AND AVOCADO

Method

1. Boil the chicken and shred it with a fork. Reserve the broth.
2. Sauté the onion, garlic, and chili. Add diced tomatoes and cook down.
3. Pour in the chicken broth, add the shredded chicken, and corn. Cook for 10 minutes.
4. Ladle the soup into bowls. Top each serving with diced avocado, fresh cilantro, and a squeeze of lime juice.

Ingredients

- Chicken breast (200g / 7 oz), canned corn (80g / 2.8 oz), 1/2 avocado, tomatoes, onion, garlic, chili pepper, cilantro, lime juice.

Macros

~500 kcal | Protein: 40g | Fat: 25g | Carbs: 28g

QUICK CANNED FISH AND EGG SOUP

Method

1. Dice the potatoes, then cover them with 600ml (2.5 cups) of water, and begin cooking.
2. Grate the carrot and chop the onion. Add to the pot.
3. When the potatoes are almost tender (10-15 mins), add the fish and mash it with a fork. Add the bay leaf.
4. Dice the hard-boiled eggs.
5. Add the eggs and plenty of fresh dill to the soup, then season to taste with salt and pepper. Remove from the heat.

Ingredients

- Canned fish in water (e.g., mackerel, salmon) (1 can, ~240g / 8.5 oz), two hard-boiled eggs, two potatoes, one carrot, 1/2 onion, fresh dill, and a bay leaf.

Macros

~460 kcal | Protein: 40g | Fat: 22g | Carbs: 25g

HUNGARIAN GOULASH SOUP WITH BEEF
(HIGH-PROTEIN ADAPTATION)

Method

1. Cube the beef and brown it in a pot.
2. Add chopped onion and carrot and sauté. Then add tomato paste, paprika, caraway, and garlic.
3. Cover with water or broth. Simmer for 1 to 1.5 hours, or until the meat is tender and falling apart.
4. Add the chopped bell pepper and cook for an additional 15 minutes.

Ingredients

- Beef (chuck or shank, 250g / 8.8 oz), one bell pepper, onion, carrot, garlic, 1 tbsp tomato paste, sweet & smoked paprika, caraway seeds.

Macros

~540 kcal | Protein: 45g | Fat: 28g | Carbs: 25g

THAI TOM YUM SOUP WITH SHRIMP
(SIMPLIFIED VERSION)

Method

1. In a pot, lightly sauté chopped onion, garlic, ginger, and chili. Add the Tom Yum paste and heat for a minute.
2. Pour in 400ml (1.7 cups) of water and bring to a boil. Add sliced mushrooms and tomatoes, and cook for 5 minutes.
3. Add the shrimp and cook for another 2-3 minutes.
4. Stir in the coconut milk, lime juice, and cilantro. Do not boil.

Ingredients

- Large shrimp (150g / 5.3 oz), mushrooms (100g / 3.5 oz), 1 tbsp Tom Yum paste, coconut milk (100ml / 0.4 cups), cherry tomatoes, onion, garlic, ginger, chili, cilantro, lime juice.

Macros

~480 kcal | Protein: 38g | Fat: 28g | Carbs: 20g

CREAMY BROCCOLI CHEDDAR SOUP WITH CHICKEN

Method

1. Boil the chicken, remove it from the broth, and dice it.
2. In the same broth, cook the broccoli, onion, and garlic until tender (7-10 minutes).
3. Blend the soup until smooth. Return to low heat.
4. Stir in the grated cheese and cream until the cheese is melted.
5. Add the diced chicken to the soup when serving.

Ingredients

- Chicken breast (150g / 5.3 oz), broccoli (250g / 8.8 oz), cheddar cheese (50g / 1.8 oz), onion, garlic, 10% cream (50ml / 0.2 cups).

Macros

~500 kcal | Protein: 42g | Fat: 30g | Carbs: 15g

HIGH-PROTEIN TURKEY CHILI

Method

1. In a large pot, brown the ground turkey.
2. Add chopped onion, garlic, and bell pepper, and cook until soft.
3. Stir in all the spices and heat for 1 minute until fragrant.
4. Add the tomatoes, rinsed beans, corn, and 200ml (0.8 cups) of water or broth.
5. Bring to a boil, then reduce the heat and simmer for 20-30 minutes to let the flavors meld. Serve with a dollop of Greek yogurt.

Ingredients

- Ground turkey (180g / 6.5 oz), canned black beans (150g / 5.3 oz), canned corn (80g / 2.8 oz), diced tomatoes (200g / 7 oz), onion, garlic, bell pepper, chili powder, cumin, smoked paprika, oregano.

Macros

~530 kcal | Protein: 45g | Fat: 20g | Carbs: 40g

PROTEIN BURGERS

The burger is America's favorite food, and now it's your secret weapon for hitting protein goals. These aren't your typical fast-food burgers—each one is engineered to deliver 32+ grams of high-quality protein while keeping you satisfied and energized. We've upgraded every component: protein-rich buns, substantial patties, and power-packed toppings that turn a simple burger into a nutritional powerhouse.

CLASSIC PROTEIN BURGER

Method

1. Season the ground beef with salt, pepper, and garlic powder. Form into one large patty.
2. Cook the patty in a hot skillet for 4-5 minutes per side, or until it reaches medium doneness.
3. In the last minute, top with cheddar cheese to melt.
4. Fry the egg sunny-side up in the same pan.
5. Assembly: Bottom bun + yogurt mayo + lettuce + tomato + cheese-topped patty + fried egg + red onion + top bun.

Ingredients

- Patty: Ground Beef (85/15): 180g / 6.5 oz
- Bun: Protein burger bun (almond flour-based)
- Toppings: Cheddar Cheese slice (30g); Fried Egg (1 large); Lettuce, Tomato, Red Onion
- Sauce: Greek Yogurt Mayo (2 tbsp Greek yogurt + 1 tbsp mayo + garlic powder)

Macros

✔ **~650 kcal | P: 48g | F: 42g | C: 18g**

TURKEY AVOCADO POWER BURGER

Method

1. Mix ground turkey with salt, pepper, cumin, and a touch of olive oil to prevent it from drying out.
2. Form into a large patty and cook for 5-6 minutes per side, until fully cooked (internal temperature of 165°F).
3. Add Swiss cheese in the last minute to melt.
4. Assembly: Bottom bun + chipotle yogurt sauce + sprouts + cheese-topped turkey patty + sliced avocado + tomato + top bun.

Ingredients

- Patty: Ground Turkey (93/7): 200g / 7 oz
- Bun: Whole-grain protein bun
- Toppings: Avocado (1/2, sliced); Swiss Cheese (30g); Sprouts; Tomato
- Sauce: Chipotle Greek Yogurt (3 tbsp Greek yogurt + 1 tsp chipotle powder + lime juice)

Macros

✔ **~620 kcal | P: 45g | F: 38g | C: 20g**

SALMON POWER BURGER

Method

1. Roughly chop the salmon fillet with a knife (don't use a food processor—you want texture).
2. Season with salt, pepper, and a touch of lemon zest. Form into a patty.
3. Cook in a hot, oiled skillet for 3-4 mins per side until just cooked through.
4. Assembly: Bottom bun + dill yogurt sauce + cucumber ribbons + salmon patty + cream cheese + red onion + capers + top bun.

Ingredients

- Patty: Fresh Salmon Fillet, skin removed: 180g / 6.5 oz
- Bun: Almond flour protein bun
- Toppings: Cream Cheese (2 tbsp); Cucumber ribbons; Red Onion; Capers
- Sauce: Dill Greek Yogurt (3 tbsp Greek yogurt + fresh dill + lemon juice)

Macros

✔ **~580 kcal | P: 42g | F: 35g | C: 18g**

CHICKEN PARMESAN BURGER

Method

1. Mix ground chicken with Italian seasoning, salt, and pepper. Form into a patty.
2. Dip the patty in beaten egg, then coat with the almond flour/Parmesan mixture.
3. Pan-fry for 5-6 mins per side until golden and cooked through.
4. Top with marinara sauce and mozzarella; cover the pan briefly to melt the cheese.
5. Assembly: Bottom bun + fresh basil + chicken parmesan patty + more marinara + top bun.

Ingredients

- Patty: Ground Chicken: 200g / 7 oz
- Bun: Whole-grain protein bun
- Coating: Almond Flour (2 tbsp); Parmesan, grated (2 tbsp)
- Toppings: Mozzarella slice (40g); Marinara Sauce (2 tbsp); Fresh Basil
- Egg for coating: 1, beaten

Macros

✔ **~680 kcal | P: 52g | F: 42g | C: 22g**

BLACK BEAN VEGGIE POWER BURGER

Method

1. Mash black beans in a bowl, leaving some texture. Mix in protein powder, almond flour, egg, diced onion, cumin, and chili powder.
2. Form into a patty and refrigerate for 15 mins to firm up.
3. Pan-fry in oil for 4-5 mins per side until crispy outside and heated through.
4. Top with pepper jack cheese in the last minute.
5. Assembly: Bottom bun + spicy mayo + sprouts + cheese-topped veggie patty + avocado + top bun.

Ingredients

- Patty Base: Canned Black Beans, mashed: 150g / 5.3 oz
- Protein Boost: Plant Protein Powder (unflavored): 20g; Almond Flour: 3 tbsp
- Binders: Egg: 1; Onion, finely diced: 1/4
- Bun: Sprouted grain protein bun
- Toppings: Pepper Jack Cheese (30g); Avocado (1/2); Sprouts
- Sauce: Spicy Mayo (2 tbsp mayo + sriracha)

Macros

~590 kcal | P: 32g | F: 28g | C: 45g

BBQ PULLED PORK BURGER

Method

1. Preparation: Use pre-cooked pulled pork (slow-cooked, leftover, or store-bought).
2. Heat the pulled pork in a skillet with the sugar-free BBQ sauce until warmed through and coated in the sauce.
3. Make quick coleslaw: shredded cabbage, Greek yogurt, apple cider vinegar, and salt.
4. Assembly: Bottom bun + coleslaw + BBQ pulled pork + cheddar cheese + pickles + almond flour onion strings + top bun.

Ingredients

- Pulled Pork: Pork Shoulder, cooked and shredded: 180g / 6.5 oz
- BBQ Sauce: Sugar-free BBQ sauce: 3 tbsp
- Bun: Almond flour protein bun
- Toppings: Coleslaw (cabbage + Greek yogurt dressing); Cheddar Cheese (30g); Pickles
- Extra Protein: Fried Onion Strings made with almond flour

Macros

~720 kcal | P: 50g | F: 48g | C: 25g

PROTEIN PIZZA

Pizza night just got a significant upgrade. These aren't your typical carb-heavy pizzas that leave you sluggish and hungry an hour later. Each recipe transforms the beloved pizza into a high-protein powerhouse using protein-rich crusts, generous cheese, and strategic toppings. Every personal-sized pizza delivers 32+ grams of protein while satisfying your deepest pizza cravings.

MARGHERITA PROTEIN PIZZA

Method

1. Crust: Microwave mozzarella and cream cheese for 1 min. Mix with almond flour and egg until a smooth dough forms.
2. Roll the dough between two pieces of parchment paper into a 10-inch circle. Bake at 425°F (220°C) for 8-10 mins until golden.
3. Spread marinara sauce, then dollops of herbed ricotta.
4. Top with fresh mozzarella, cherry tomatoes, and Parmesan.
5. Bake for 8-10 mins until cheese is bubbly. Garnish with fresh basil.

Ingredients

- Crust: Mozzarella, shredded (100g); Almond Flour (60g); Cream Cheese (30g); Egg (1)
- Sauce: Marinara (low-sugar): 3 tbsp
- Toppings: Fresh Mozzarella, sliced (80g); Parmesan, grated (20g); Fresh Basil; Cherry Tomatoes, halved
- Protein Boost: Ricotta Cheese (60g) mixed with Italian herbs

Macros

~580 kcal | P: 38g | F: 42g | C: 12g

MEAT LOVERS PROTEIN PIZZA

Method

1. Prepare and pre-bake the fathead crust as above.
2. Spread pizza sauce evenly over the crust.
3. Layer with half the mozzarella, then all the meats, then the remaining mozzarella and cheddar.
4. Bake at 425°F (220°C) for 10-12 mins until cheese is golden and bubbly.
5. Let cool for 5 mins before slicing to prevent the cheese from sliding off.

Ingredients

- Crust: Same fathead dough as above
- Sauce: Pizza sauce (low-sugar): 3 tbsp
- Meats: Pepperoni, sliced (40g); Italian Sausage, cooked & crumbled (60g); Bacon, cooked & chopped (30g)
- Cheese: Mozzarella, shredded (100g); Cheddar, shredded (40g)

Macros

~720 kcal | P: 52g | F: 55g | C: 10g

BBQ CHICKEN PROTEIN PIZZA

Method

1. Prepare and pre-bake the fathead crust.
2. Spread BBQ sauce over the crust, leaving a 1-inch border.
3. Top with half the mozzarella, then diced chicken, red onion, and remaining cheeses.
4. Bake at 425°F (220°C) for 10-12 minutes, until the cheese has melted and the edges are golden brown.
5. Drizzle with ranch Greek yogurt and garnish with fresh cilantro.

Ingredients

- Crust: Same fathead dough as above
- Sauce: Sugar-free BBQ sauce: 4 tbsp
- Protein: Cooked Chicken Breast, diced (120g); Mozzarella, shredded (80g); Gouda, shredded (40g)
- Toppings: Red Onion, thinly sliced; Cilantro, chopped
- Extra: Greek Yogurt (2 tbsp) mixed with ranch seasoning for drizzle

Macros

~650 kcal | P: 48g | F: 40g | C: 18g

MEDITERRANEAN PROTEIN PIZZA

Method

1. Prepare and pre-bake the fathead crust.
2. Spread the herbed ricotta mixture as the base sauce.
3. Top with spinach leaves, sun-dried tomatoes, red onion, and olives.
4. Sprinkle with mozzarella and feta cheeses, then pine nuts.
5. Bake at 425°F (220°C) for 10-12 mins. Finish with fresh oregano.

Ingredients

- Crust: Same fathead dough as above
- Base: Ricotta Cheese (80g) mixed with garlic and herbs
- Proteins: Feta Cheese, crumbled (60g); Mozzarella, shredded (60g)
- Toppings: Kalamata Olives, pitted & halved; Sun-dried Tomatoes; Red Onion; Spinach leaves
- Finish: Pine Nuts (1 tbsp); Fresh Oregano

Macros

~620 kcal | P: 42g | F: 45g | C: 15g

BREAKFAST PROTEIN PIZZA

Method

1. Prepare and pre-bake the fathead crust.
2. Spread the herbed Greek yogurt as the base.
3. Top with half the cheese, then scrambled eggs, sausage, and bacon.
4. Add cherry tomatoes and remaining cheese.
5. Bake at 425°F (220°C) for 8-10 mins until cheese melts.
6. Garnish with green onions before serving.

Ingredients

- Crust: Same fathead dough as above
- Base: Greek Yogurt (3 tbsp) mixed with garlic powder and herbs
- Proteins: Scrambled Eggs (2 large); Breakfast Sausage, cooked & crumbled (60g); Bacon, chopped (30g)
- Cheese: Cheddar, shredded (80g); Mozzarella, shredded (40g)
- Toppings: Green Onions, sliced; Cherry Tomatoes, halved

Macros

~680 kcal | P: 45g | F: 50g | C: 12g

Protein Pizza Success Tips:

1. Pre-bake the Crust: Always pre-bake your protein crust for 8-10 minutes before adding toppings to prevent sogginess.
2. Cheese Strategy: Use a mix of cheeses for both flavor and protein. Mozzarella melts beautifully, while harder cheeses add protein density.
3. Don't Overload: Too many toppings will make the crust soggy. Less is more for the perfect protein pizza.
4. Let It Rest: Allow the pizza to cool for 5 minutes after baking. This helps the cheese set and makes slicing easier.
5. Make-Ahead Crusts: Fathead dough can be refrigerated for up to 3 days or frozen for up to 1 month.

PROTEIN DESSERTS

Who says you can't have your cake and eat it too? These desserts prove that sweet treats can be both indulgent and nutritious. Each recipe delivers 15-25 grams of high-quality protein while satisfying your deepest cravings for a sweet treat. No more guilt, no more derailed diets—just pure, protein-packed pleasure.

PROTEIN CHOCOLATE MOUSSE

Method

1. In a bowl, whisk together protein powder, cocoa powder, and sweetener.
2. Add Greek yogurt and vanilla extract. Mix until smooth.
3. Gradually add heavy cream, whisking until the mixture reaches a light, mousse-like consistency.
4. Taste and adjust sweetness as needed.
5. Chill for at least 30 minutes. Serve garnished with grated dark chocolate.

Ingredients

- Greek Yogurt (plain): 150g / 5.3 oz
- Chocolate Protein Powder: 30g / 1 oz
- Unsweetened Cocoa Powder: 2 tbsp
- Erythritol or Stevia: to taste (about 2-3 tsp)
- Vanilla Extract: 1/2 tsp
- Heavy Cream: 2 tbsp
- Dark Chocolate (85%+), grated: 1 tsp for garnish

Macros

~280 kcal | P: 22g | F: 18g | C: 8g

HIGH-PROTEIN MINI CHEESECAKE

Method

1. Preheat oven to 325°F (160°C). Line a large muffin cup or small ramekin.
2. Crust: Mix almond flour, melted butter, and erythritol. Press into the bottom of the muffin cup.
3. Filling: Beat cream cheese until smooth. Add Greek yogurt, protein powder, egg, vanilla, and lemon zest. Mix until creamy.
4. Pour filling over the crust.
5. Bake for 20-25 minutes until set but still slightly jiggly in the center.
6. Cool completely, then refrigerate for at least 2 hours. Top with berries before serving.

Ingredients

- Crust: Almond Flour (3 tbsp), Melted Butter (1 tbsp), Erythritol (1 tsp)
- Filling: Cream Cheese, softened (60g), Greek Yogurt (100g), Vanilla Protein Powder (25g), Egg (1 small), Vanilla Extract, Lemon Zest
- Topping: Fresh berries (optional)

Macros

~320 kcal | P: 25g | F: 20g | C: 12g

PROTEIN COOKIE DOUGH BITES

Method

1. In a bowl, mix protein powder, almond flour, erythritol, and salt.
2. Add almond butter and vanilla extract. Mix until combined.
3. Add almond milk gradually until the mixture holds together like cookie dough.
4. Fold in chocolate chips.
5. Roll into eight small balls. Chill for 30 minutes to allow the mixture to firm up.
6. Store in the refrigerator for up to 1 week.

Ingredients

- Vanilla Protein Powder: 30g / 1 oz
- Almond Flour: 3 tbsp
- Natural Almond Butter: 2 tbsp
- Erythritol: 1-2 tsp
- Vanilla Extract: 1/2 tsp
- Salt: pinch
- Sugar-Free Chocolate Chips: 1 tbsp
- Almond Milk: 1-2 tbsp (as needed)

Macros

~290 kcal | P: 20g | F: 18g | C: 10g

GREEK YOGURT BERRY POWER PARFAIT

Method

1. In a bowl, mix Greek yogurt with protein powder until smooth.
2. If using frozen berries, thaw them slightly and mash lightly to release juices.
3. Assembly: In a glass or bowl, layer half the protein yogurt, then berries, then the remaining yogurt.
4. Top with chopped almonds and chia seeds.
5. Drizzle with honey or sugar-free syrup and sprinkle with cinnamon.
6. Serve immediately or chill for up to 2 hours.

Ingredients

- Greek Yogurt (plain): 200g / 7 oz
- Vanilla Protein Powder: 15g / 0.5 oz
- Mixed Berries (fresh or frozen): 80g / 2.8 oz
- Chopped Almonds: 2 tbsp
- Chia Seeds: 1 tbsp
- Honey or Sugar-Free Syrup: 1 tsp
- Cinnamon: pinch

Macros

~310 kcal | P: 24g | F: 15g | C: 18g

PROTEIN FUDGE BROWNIES

Method

1. Preheat oven to 350°F (175°C). Line a small 6x6-inch baking dish with parchment paper.
2. In a bowl, whisk together protein powder, almond flour, cocoa powder, erythritol, baking powder, and salt.
3. In another bowl, beat eggs, almond butter, and vanilla until smooth.
4. Combine wet and dry ingredients. Fold in chocolate chips.
5. Pour into the prepared baking dish and spread evenly.
6. Bake for 18-22 minutes until a toothpick comes out with a few moist crumbs.
7. Cool completely before cutting into four squares.

Ingredients

- Chocolate Protein Powder: 60g / 2 oz
- Almond Flour: 4 tbsp
- Unsweetened Cocoa Powder: 2 tbsp
- Erythritol: 3 tbsp
- Eggs: 2 large
- Natural Almond Butter: 3 tbsp
- Vanilla Extract: 1 tsp
- Baking Powder: 1/2 tsp
- Salt: pinch
- Sugar-Free Chocolate Chips: 2 tbsp

Macros

~250 kcal | P: 18g | F: 16g | C: 8g

PEANUT BUTTER PROTEIN POWER BALLS

Method

1. In a bowl, mix peanut butter, protein powder, oats, chia seeds, erythritol, vanilla, and salt.
2. Stir until the mixture holds together. If too dry, add 1-2 tsp water.
3. Roll the mixture into intonine9 small balls (about 1 inch diameter).
4. Roll each ball in coconut flakes to coat.
5. Place on a plate and refrigerate for at least 1 hour to firm up.
6. Store in the refrigerator for up to 1 week.

Ingredients

- Natural Peanut Butter: 4 tbsp
- Vanilla Protein Powder: 40g / 1.4 oz
- Rolled Oats (old-fashioned): 3 tbsp
- Chia Seeds: 1 tbsp
- Erythritol: 1-2 tsp
- Vanilla Extract: 1/2 tsp
- Salt: pinch; Unsweetened Coconut Flakes: 2 tbsp (for rolling)

Macros

~320 kcal | P: 22g | F: 22g | C: 8g

REFERENCE MATERIALS

SAUCES & MARINADES

Universal High-Protein Sauces

Greek Yogurt Base Sauces (8-12g protein per serving)

- Garlic Herb: Greek yogurt + minced garlic + dill + lemon juice
- Chipotle: Greek yogurt + chipotle powder + lime juice + honey substitute
- Ranch: Greek yogurt + ranch seasoning packet + splash of milk
- Tzatziki: Greek yogurt + grated cucumber + garlic + dill + salt

Nut & Seed Sauces (6-10g protein per serving)

- Tahini Dressing: Tahini + lemon juice + garlic + water to thin
- Almond Satay: Almond butter + soy sauce + rice vinegar + sriracha
- Cashew Cream: Soaked cashews + water + lemon juice + salt (blend smooth)
- Pesto Power: Basil + pine nuts + parmesan + olive oil + garlic

MARINADES BY PROTEIN TYPE

Chicken/Turkey

- Asian: Soy sauce + sesame oil + ginger + garlic + rice vinegar
- Mediterranean: Olive oil + lemon juice + oregano + garlic + salt
- Mexican: Lime juice + cumin + chili powder + garlic + cilantro

Beef/Lamb

- Korean: Soy sauce + sesame oil + pear juice + garlic + ginger
- Middle Eastern: Olive oil + lemon juice + sumac + allspice + onion
- American: Worcestershire + garlic + black pepper + olive oil

Fish/Seafood

- Lemon Herb: Olive oil + lemon juice + thyme + parsley + garlic
- Asian: Soy sauce + mirin + ginger + green onion
- Cajun: Olive oil + paprika + cayenne + garlic + oregano

GLOBAL SPICE COMBINATIONS

Cuisine	Essential Spices	Ratio
Indian	Turmeric, cumin, coriander, garam masala	1:2:2:1
Mexican	Cumin, chili powder, paprika, oregano	2:3:1:1
Middle Eastern	Sumac, za'atar, allspice, cinnamon	2:1:1:0.5
Asian	Five-spice, ginger powder, garlic powder	1:1:2
Mediterranean	Oregano, basil, thyme, rosemary	2:1:1:1

FIBER & CARB GUIDE

HIGH-FIBER VEGETABLES CONTENT TABLE (PER 100G COOKED)

Vegetable	Fiber (g)	Net Carbs (g)	Best Use
Artichoke	8.6	2.4	Salads, sides
Brussels Sprouts	4.1	3.5	Roasted, stir-fry
Broccoli	3.3	2.4	Universal
Cauliflower	2.3	2.0	Rice substitute
Spinach	2.4	1.4	Salads, cooking
Asparagus	2.1	1.9	Grilled, steamed
Cabbage	2.3	3.2	Slaws, wraps
Bell Peppers	1.7	4.3	Stir-fry, raw

CARB SUBSTITUTION SYSTEM WITH MACROS

4-Level Carb System

Level 1: Ultra Low-Carb (<15g)

- Sides: Cauliflower rice, zucchini noodles, sautéed spinach
- Portions: 200g cooked vegetables
- Fiber Goal: 8-12g

Level 2: Low-Carb (<30g)

- Sides: Roasted broccoli, Brussels sprouts, asparagus
- Portions: 250g cooked vegetables
- Fiber Goal: 10-15g

Level 3: Moderate-Carb (<50g)

- Sides: 1/2 cup quinoa, lentils, or sweet potato + vegetables
- Portions: 100g grains/legumes + 150g vegetables
- Fiber Goal: 12-18g

Level 4: High-Carb (50g+)

- Sides: 1 cup brown rice, oats, or beans + vegetables
- Portions: 200g grains/legumes + 100g vegetables
- Fiber Goal: 15-25g

How to increase fiber without changing taste

Fiber Boosters (Add to any dish)

- Chia Seeds: 1 tbsp = 5g fiber
- Ground Flaxseed: 1 tbsp = 3g fiber
- Psyllium Husk: 1 tsp = 4g fiber
- Hemp Hearts: 1 tbsp = 1g fiber + 3g protein

MEAL PREP & BATCH COOKING

BATCH COOKING STRATEGIES FOR HIGH-PROTEIN DISHES

Sunday Prep

1. Slow Cooker: Start pulled pork or chicken (4-6 hours)
2. Oven: Bake chicken breasts, roast vegetables (1 hour)
3. Stovetop: Cook ground meat, hard-boil eggs (30 mins)
4. Prep: Wash/chop vegetables, portion snacks

Storage Times

- Cooked Chicken/Turkey: 4 days refrigerated, 3 months frozen
- Cooked Beef/Pork: 4 days refrigerated, 4 months frozen
- Cooked Fish: 2 days refrigerated, 2 months frozen
- Eggs (cooked): 7 days refrigerated
- Cut Vegetables: 3-5 days refrigerated

Container System

- Glass containers: Hot foods, reheating
- BPA-free plastic: Cold salads, snacks
- Mason jars: Dressings, overnight oats
- Freezer bags: Bulk proteins, smoothie packs

MEAL PREP STRATEGIES

Salad Prep (5-day freshness)

1. Bottom: Dressing in a separate container
2. Layer 1: Hard vegetables (carrots, peppers)
3. Layer 2: Proteins (chicken, eggs, cheese)
4. Layer 3: Soft vegetables (tomatoes, cucumber)
5. Top: Greens and delicate herbs

Burger/Pizza Prep

- Patties: Form and freeze with parchment between
- Pizza Crusts: Pre-bake and freeze for up to 3 months
- Toppings: Prep and store separately, assemble when ready

Curry/Stew Storage

- Cool completely before refrigerating
- Freeze in portions for up to 6 months
- Add fresh herbs after reheating
- Thin with broth if too thick after storage

COOKING MEASUREMENT CONVERSION TABLE

VOLUME

US (cups/spoons)	UK (ml)	Metric (ml)
1 cup	240 ml	250 ml*
3/4 cup	180 ml	180 ml
2/3 cup	160 ml	160 ml
1/2 cup	120 ml	125 ml
1/3 cup	80 ml	80 ml
1/4 cup	60 ml	60 ml
1 tbsp (tablespoon)	15 ml	15 ml
1 tsp (teaspoon)	5 ml	5 ml
1/2 tsp	2.5 ml	2.5 ml

WEIGHT

US/UK	Metric (grams)
1 oz (ounce)	28 g
2 oz	55 g
4 oz (1/4 lb)	113 g
8 oz (1/2 lb)	227 g
16 oz (1 lb)	454 g

LIQUIDS

US/UK	Metric (liters)	
1 fl oz (fluid ounce)	30 ml	
8 fl oz (1 cup)	240 ml	
16 fl oz (1 pint US)	473 ml	UK pint = 568 ml
32 fl oz (1 quart US)	946 ml	UK quart = 1,13 l
128 fl oz (1 gallon US)	3.78 l	UK gallon = 4.54 l

TEMPERATURES

Fahrenheit (°F)	Celsius (°C)
250 °F	120 °C
300 °F	150 °C
325 °F	160 °C
350 °F	175 °C
375 °F	190 °C
400 °F	200 °C
425 °F	220 °C
450 °F	230 °C

SEBASTIAN HARTWELL

About the author

Sebastian Hartwell is an integrative health researcher and human performance specialist with expertise in metabolic health, nutrition science, and performance optimization. His international work allows him to study and apply global best practices in nutrition.
Professional Background: Hartwell works with professional athletes, executives, and high-performance individuals worldwide, developing evidence-based nutrition protocols for sustainable health goals. His research focuses on metabolic flexibility, protein optimization, and practical nutrition strategies.

Culinary Philosophy: Through years of client work across cultures, Hartwell discovered the most significant barrier to high-protein diets was flavor fatigue, not knowledge. This cookbook delivers internationally-inspired recipes with precise protein targets and exceptional taste.

Areas of Expertise:

- Metabolic health and protein utilization optimization
- Sports nutrition and muscle-building protocols
- International cuisine adaptation for health goals
- Low-carb and ketogenic nutrition approaches
- GLP-1 medication dietary support

Philosophy: "Optimal nutrition doesn't require bland meals. My goal is evidence-based recipes that create sustainable transformation through delicious, practical daily nutrition."

Hartwell continues to develop practical nutrition protocols, tested internationally with people from diverse cultures and lifestyles.

> *I'm incredibly grateful that you chose to cook with me through these pages!*
> *It's been such a joy to share these recipes with you, and I hope they've brought you some great meals. If this cookbook has been helpful to you, I would really appreciate your review. Your thoughts mean a great deal to me.*
> — Sebastian

OTHER BOOKS BY SEBASTIAN HARTWELL

High-Protein After GLP-1 Cookbook
110+ Low-Carb, Keto-Friendly Recipes to Maintain Weight Loss, Burn Fat, and Curb Appetite for Ozempic, GLP-1, and Semaglutide Users After Treatment

21-DAY PROGRAM SERIES 6 BOOK

1. The 21-Day Insomnia Solution.
How to Fall Asleep Fast, Beat Sleep Anxiety Naturally Without Pills: A Science-Backed Program to Wake Up Refreshed

2. Stop Anxiety and Overthinking in 21 Days
A 21-Day Program to Stop Overthinking, Calm Your Mind, Break the Cycle of Worry, Ease Stress, Improve Emotional Balance, and Build Lasting Mental Clarity Through Mindfulness and Daily Habits

3. Digital Detox
How to Reduce Screen Time, Break Free from Phone and Social Media Addiction, Overcome Tech Burnout, Reclaim Focus, Improve Mental Health, and Create a Balanced, Mindful Digital Life

4. Cortisol Detox
A 21-Day Hormone Reset Program to Naturally Lower Cortisol, Recover from Adrenal Fatigue, Improve Sleep Quality, and Burn Belly Fat with Anti-Inflammatory Recipes and Sustainable Lifestyle Habits

5. Biohacking for Women
A 21-Day Program to Balance Hormones Naturally, Boost Energy and Mood, Improve Focus and Skin, Support Healthy Weight Loss, Promote Anti-Aging, and Strengthen Women's Health Through Smart Nutrition and Daily Lifestyle Habits.

6. Biohacking for Men
A 21-Day Program to Support Healthy Testosterone and Libido, Boost Energy and Focus, Improve Sleep, Burn Fat, and Optimize Strength, Longevity, and Men's Health Through Smart Nutrition and Lifestyle Habits.

DISCLAIMER
Medical Advice: This book is for informational purposes only. Consult your doctor before making any changes to your diet, especially if you have underlying health conditions or are taking medications.
Nutritional Information: Macro calculations are estimates. Actual values may vary depending on the ingredients and preparation methods used.
Food Safety: You are responsible for checking ingredient lists for potential allergens and following proper food safety practices.
Results: Individual results will vary. No guarantees are made regarding weight loss, muscle gain, or health outcomes.
Supplements: Use protein powders and supplements at your own discretion. Read labels and consult healthcare providers.
Liability: The author and publisher disclaim any liability for adverse effects resulting from the use of these recipes.

ISBN 978-3-907779-00-2
Publisher: EruditPress
Email: contact@eruditpress.com

Printed in Dunstable, United Kingdom

76446497R00051